Children and Psychologists

Phillip Williams

HODDER AND STOUGHTON
LONDON SYDNEY AUCKLAND TORONTO

ISBN 0 340 21942 4

First published 1977
Copyright © 1977 Phillip Williams and National Children's Home

Printed and bound in Great Britain for Hodder and Stoughton Educational, a
division of Hodder and Stoughton Ltd, Mill Road, Dunton Green, Sevenoaks, Kent,
by The Benham Press, William Clowes & Sons Ltd, Colchester, Beccles and London.

Contents

List of Figures and Tables   iv

Acknowledgments   v

Preface   vii

Chapter 1   Why study children?   1

        2   How children are studied   15

        3   Children's behaviour   28

        4   Influences on development   40

        5   Working with children, 1   49

        6   Working with children, 2   66

        7   The professions of child psychology   75

References   81

Index   87

List of Figures and Tables

Figure 1   The growth of de Montbeillard's son   16

2   The growth of word recognition skills   24, 25
(a) A cross-sectional study
(b) A longitudinal study, Case A
(c) A longitudinal study, Case D

3   Variation in 'worrying' behaviour with age   36

4   Regional treatment rates at child guidance clinics   39

5   Frequency of contact between educational psychologists and other services   52

6   A section of a children's behaviour questionnaire   54–5

7   Example of details of a child's history   55–7

8   Educational psychologists in England and Wales, 1955–75   67

Table I   Estimates of 'half-development' of selected characteristics   8

II   A grouping of symptoms which may be indicative of maladjustment   31

III   Percentages of children recorded as showing extreme types of behaviour   33

IV   Scheme for rating children's behaviour   35

V   The relationship between the number of deviant behaviour items underlined by parents and the number of behaviour problems underlined by teachers   37

Acknowledgments

The author and publishers would like to thank the following for permission to reproduce copyright material:
Addison-Wesley Publishing Co. for a passage reprinted by special permission from Joseph Perez, from *Counseling: Theory and Practice* (1965) Addison-Wesley, Reading, Mass.; Basil Blackwell and Mott Ltd for three graphs taken from *Aspects of Early Reading Growth* (pages 14, 16 and 17) by Pat Davies and Phillip Williams; Robert Gibson and Sons, Glasgow, Ltd for a passage from the instructions in the *Manual to Kelvin Measurement of Ability in Infant Classes* by C. M. Fleming; the Controller of Her Majesty's Stationery Office for a map and also a diagram based on figure 2.9 and table 2B.19, both from *Psychologists in Education Services* (Summerfield Report), and for a table from the *Report of the Committee on Maladjusted Children* (Underwood Report); Hodder and Stoughton Ltd on behalf of Professor Michael Shepherd and his co-authors for a figure (36), two tables (6 and 31) and a section of Appendix 3 from their *Childhood Behaviour and Mental Health*; Houghton Mifflin Company for a passage reprinted from *Dibs: in search of self* by Virginia M. Axline (copyright © 1964 by Virginia M. Axline and used by permission of Houghton Mifflin Company), also Victor Gollancz Ltd as publisher of the British edition; the Longman Group Ltd for various items reprinted from *The Practice of Educational Psychology* edited by M. Chazan *et al.*, namely a passage from H. J. Wright's contribution 'Principles in practice' and the example of details from a child's history from T. Moore's contribution 'The educational psychologist and parents', also the graph showing educational psychologists in England and Wales prepared by Phillip Williams for his contribution 'The growth and scope of the school psychological service'; The Open

University for the extract from its course P853, Unit 3, 'Growing up with a disability' by Peter Mittler; Routledge and Kegan Paul for a passage from *Growth of Logical Thinking from Childhood to Adolescence* by J. Piaget and B. Inhelder, translated by A. Parsons and S. Milgram, © 1958 by Basic Books Inc., Publisher, New York; Scottish Academic Press Ltd for permission to make use of a table based on an article 'Teachers' ratings of classroom behaviour' by G. W. Herbert, originally published in the *British Journal of Educational Psychology*, 1974, 44, 3; Professor Howard N. Sloane, Jr, deviser of the programme which is here reproduced on pages 59–60.

The author and publisher are also grateful to Colin Smythe Ltd on behalf of the AE Estate for permission to quote at the head of Chapter 1 six lines from 'Germinal', and to Faber and Faber Ltd and Oxford University Press, New York, for permission to quote at the head of Chapter 3 five lines from 'The Habits' from *The Collected Poems of Louis MacNeice*.

Preface

When the National Children's Home invited me to give the 1976 Convocation Lecture, I responded with pleasure, and for a variety of reasons, not least of which was the opportunity to speak on any topic I chose. In the event the choice proved less easy than I had thought; most of us own several hobby-horses and the wish to ride two or more simultaneously must be curbed.

Eventually, I chose to try to tackle a fairly broad theme—the ways in which applied psychologists work with children and the kinds of skills they offer to a society which is increasingly aware of their activities, but not always well-informed about them. This topic excludes much discussion of the related and important area of research in child development and behaviour. Nevertheless, it is still sufficiently broad for me to be glad to have the chance of expanding the material of the lecture into this small book.

Few professions have grown as rapidly in recent years as applied psychology. In the early 1950s there were just over a hundred educational psychologists employed in England and Wales. Twenty-five years later there were approximately a thousand educational psychologists in post, a tenfold increase. But not only have the numbers of educational psychologists grown; other groups of applied psychologists are increasingly interested in the psychology of childhood—social psychologists, clinical psychologists, developmental psychologists, and so on. Not only is the range of specialisms growing, so is the size of each. Thus there were in 1973 over four hundred clinical psychologists working in Great Britain, of whom a sizeable proportion specialized in work with children.

What is it that psychologists who work with children actually do? Has the term 'child psychologist' been superseded by the range of specialisms outlined above? Do we need to reinstate the 'child' in psychology? Will the growth in the numbers of applied psychologists working with children mean that roles and methods of working must change drastically? These are some of the questions on which the lecture touched and which the book tries to extend.

In doing so, the contents draw heavily but not exclusively on examples from educational psychology. Educational psychologists constitute the most numerous group of applied psychologists working with children and the group with which most readers are likely to come in contact. Educational psychology is also a very long-established discipline. But the growing importance of other specialisms must be recognized.

The book makes no pretence at weaving threads drawn from the different psychological specialisms into a text book of child psychology. That is an ambitious task which awaits another author. The purpose of the book is more modest. It seeks to depict some of the activities of applied psychologists working with children in such a way that non-psychologists—parents, teachers, doctors, social workers—will be a little more aware of the nature and extent of the psychologist's contribution to the well-being of children.

The material would not have been prepared without assistance. I want to express appreciation to John Bynner, Mary Nixon and Jack Wright who read the manuscript and commented on it. I am indebted to Iris Bennett, who arranged the typing of the final manuscript at long range, and to Brenda Madden who handled the earlier drafts. Finally, I acknowledge gratefully the support given by Gordon Barritt, Principal of the National Children's Home, both in providing helpful material before the lecture and in displaying great patience thereafter.

Melbourne,   Phillip Williams
September 1976

NOTE
The National Children's Home Convocation Lectures have been published annually since 1946 and many are still available in book form; if you are interested, please write to the National Children's Home at 85 Highbury Park, London, N5 1UD.

CHAPTER 1 | Why study children?

In ancient shadows and twilights
Where childhood had strayed
The world's great sorrows were born
And its heroes were made.
In the lost boyhood of Judas
Christ was betrayed.

From 'Germinal' by George William Russell

There was a time when the question 'What is psychology?' exercised many people, not least psychologists themselves. Many years ago a body of eminent psychologists devoted a symposium to this topic, and emerged with as many definitions of psychology as contributors. Although it is tempting to examine alternative views of the psychologist's territory, for the purposes of this book psychology can be broadly regarded as the scientific study of behaviour and child psychology as the scientific study of children's behaviour. As we shall see in later chapters, the kinds of behaviour that interest psychologists vary, and the word 'scientific' needs interpretation. But we shall return to these points.

Why do some psychologists wish to study the behaviour of children? The purpose of this chapter is to outline some answers to this question and in essence the chapter suggests that there are three main reasons. The reasons are not always distinct, they are not the only reasons, nor are they usually found singly. The motivation of psychologists is just as complicated as the motivation of others. But in order to try to simplify and so to understand a complex field, this chapter identifies three main strands in the answer to the question at the start of the paragraph.

These are:

   (i) *Understanding children and childhood*—a quest for knowledge for
       its own sake.
  (ii) *Predicting human development*—examining the relationships
       between characteristics of children and adults leads to
       attempts to forecast one from the other. It is an interest in
       predicting adult development from knowledge of children
       that gives rise to the second reason for studying childhood.
 (iii) *Influencing human development*—the third reason can be de-
       scribed as influence, deriving from application. The appli-
       cation of the knowledge of (i) and the relationships of (ii)
       enables psychologists to respond to requests to influence, to
       some extent, the course of human growth. This is another way
       of saying that the interest which psychologists display in
       behaviour extends to changing behaviour, and more parti-
       cularly to learning.

In the rest of this chapter we begin to unravel these three strands in
more detail.

(i) *Understanding childhood*

Child psychology, as a seriously established academic area, came late.
Its beginnings are often dated from Charles Darwin's 'Autobiographical Sketch of an Infant', published in the journal *Mind* in 1877. The
parentage is aristocratic, scientifically speaking, but the gestation
period was a lengthy one since the work which Darwin reported in
1877 was carried out in 1840. Its publication was soon paralleled by
similar studies in France and Germany, where Perez and Preyer
published in 1878 and 1882 respectively.

   Whether the beginning of the serious study of child psychology is
dated from 1840 or 1877, it is interesting to contrast either date with
the development of other studies of childhood, derived from other
scientific disciplines. For example, what is said to be the first book of
paediatrics published by an Englishman (*The Boke of Chyldren*, written
by Thomas Phaire) appeared in 1544. Several of the childhood
illnesses which Phaire mentioned (e.g. Terryble Dreames, Bredyng of
Teeth) would be entirely familiar today, even though the treatment he
recommended would be much less acceptable. Part of the reason for
this early appearance of a medical interest in childhood is of course the
much longer scientific tradition which medicine has enjoyed. Even so,
the appearance of Phaire's book is early, well ahead of the time.

In the years preceding the nineteenth century, childhood was not a subject for serious study. Children were not seen as the precious transmitters of the future which we think of them as today. At a time when contraception, although not unknown, was not widely practised, many children were born. But at a time when public health services were virtually non-existent, few survived. Caulfield (1931), writing of the infant welfare movement, suggests that in London in the middle of the eighteenth century 75 per cent of all children christened were dead before they were five years of age. The belief that children were provided in large numbers so that only a few might survive was widely held, and the death of an infant or young child was not viewed in the same way as we would view this event today. Montaigne wrote, 'I have lost two or three children in their infancy, not without regret, but without great sorrow' (reported in Aries, 1966). Aries expounds the view that before the seventeenth century a child was simply a small, inadequate adult. He argues that the concept of childhood as something distinct from adulthood belongs to the twentieth century, described by Key (in Kanner, 1957) as 'the century of the child'. Kanner, one of the founders of modern child psychiatry, supports this view, arguing that: 'When the twentieth century made its appearance, there was not—and there could not be—anything that might in any sense be regarded as child psychiatry.'

During the twentieth century there emerged a slow and gradual realisation that children and childhood were 'ideas' to which much greater attention could be paid. This is not to deny that there were advanced thinkers in earlier ages who had argued for the importance of childhood and its study. Rousseau and Itard are examples of educational pioneers who, in the middle of the eighteenth century and the early years of the nineteenth, had focused attention on children and their development. But the full effects of their work were not to be felt for many years afterwards and the historians of childhood argue that it was in the nineteenth century that the major shift of interest occurred. Great changes in thinking of this kind do not occur overnight. What was it in the nineteenth century which led to such a radical shift in our ideas?

Within the great changes of the nineteenth century several different threads can be detected. Perhaps the first thread was the libertarian thinking which characterised the French and American revolutions. Neglected groups of humanity were given new status. Human rights became an issue of concern which spread to the rights of children as

well as adults. The reforming zeal of individuals such as John Stuart
Mill in Britain led to a strengthening of the cry for more education for
children. The economic need for a literate and numerate population,
trained in the new skills demanded by the industrial revolution,
increased the pressure for more effort to be put into training the young,
and hence for studying the ways in which these new skills could best be
learned. The social effects of the large conurbations which sprang up in
the train of the industrial revolution also contributed to this new
theme. Thus the sight of bands of unoccupied children roaming the
streets of the industrial towns of England was a phenomenon not
observed during earlier centuries of rural life and one which led to the
recognition of need for social reform.

The main solution offered to meet these problems was a system of
compulsory education. Education itself was not of course a new
development; children had been educated since the earliest times, but
in most of the major civilizations education had been reserved for a
small élite. Education for all children represented a much newer
development, and one which many people found difficult to accept. In
an earlier lecture (1952) in this series, Cyril Burt (1957) illustrated
some of the attitudes which informed the Parliamentary debate on the
topic of universal education: 'You may train your hounds and your
pointers,' said the member for Newark in 1868, 'but never the hare or
the fox.' In spite of attitudes such as these, the view of the liberals
prevailed and a system of compulsory education for all children in this
country was introduced with the Forster Act of 1870.

This step solved many problems, but created others. The compulsory attendance of children at school, where they were aggregated into
large classes, often sixty or seventy strong, led to the newly enlarged
profession of teachers having to deal with '... urchins who could not
learn and ruffians who could not be controlled' (F. Warner, quoted in
Burt, 1957). The old system of making grants to school boards,
according to the level of attainment of the pupils, proved inadequate.
The salaries of teachers were drawn from these grants and so, where
teachers could not raise the standards of performance of their children
to those expected by the Board of Education, their salaries suffered.
This system of 'payment by results' might have been acceptable at a
time when only able and well-motivated children entered schools;
when children from adverse circumstances were taught in large
numbers, not only were the children disadvantaged—so were the
teachers.

Reasons such as these led in the last decades of the nineteenth century to the establishment of special classes for children with learning difficulties and to the consequent need to identify children who were suitable for admission to them. These questions demanded information about children's intellectual and social behaviour. But it would be wrong to think that practical issues were alone responsible for generating the development and early growth of child psychology. At this point the subject of psychology itself, then thought of as the study of the human mind, was undergoing a major change. The scientific thinking of the Victorian age was beginning to influence this field of study.

Darwin's book *The Expression of Emotions* is regarded as a landmark in this context, in part since the work he reported used the observational techniques of the natural sciences and applied them to human behaviour. This emphasis on scientific observation was soon to be allied to the development of a new kind of measurement. In short, the philosophical speculations of James Mill and Thomas Brown were giving way to modern scientific psychology. Bain, described by Hearnshaw (1964) as '... standing half way between the mental philosophy of the eighteenth and early nineteenth century and the scientific psychology of the twentieth', was a pivotal figure in this change. This conjunction of the introduction of scientific method in psychology, with the great concern with the newly-discerned problems connected with childhood, led to the child study movement being started at the end of the nineteenth century.

In much the same way, adolescence has become an area of great interest to twentieth-century psychologists. The extension of compulsory schooling into the middle and later teen-age years led to the teaching profession and the education system having to deal with young people passing from childhood into maturity. One effect of this situation has been to give great impetus to psychological studies of the adolescent, just as the introduction of compulsory schooling for young children led to the growth of the child study movements.

Hearnshaw wrote in his *Short History of British Psychology*, '... There was, in fact, an amateur flavour, not unlike that of the early birdwatchers, about the child study movement; and after the establishment of academic departments of psychology, and the evolution of research tools and techniques, it inevitably became outmoded.'

It may well have been amateurish: it was also influential. The names of the London County Council Inspectors Ballard and Winch, of Francis Galton, the pioneer of modern educational statistics, of Sully, whose laboratory for the study of children was started in University College, London, in the 1880s were some of those associated with the foundation and the early years of the Child Study Association. This body had strong educational affiliations and it included many of the early psychologists. Years later, Margaret McMillan, one of the pioneers of infant education in the nineteenth century wrote '... it is remarkable how the centre of interest has now shifted from subjects of study to the child. In those days there was little child study but there was scholarship; and this was an advantage to the child in some ways. People did not study him, but he was allowed to study.' By the end of the century the child study movement was in full swing and psychology was being transformed into a scientific discipline. It is an exaggeration to say that the history of the childhood of psychology is the history of the psychology of childhood. But it is, nevertheless, partly true.

During the last half-century the study of children's behaviour has attracted the interest and efforts of many psychologists. The acquisition of children's language structures, the pattern of relationships existing in children's groups, the development of mathematical knowledge in children, the understanding children have of adult moral and ethical values, children's patterns of motor skill, their perception of physical characteristics such as length and weight, the effect of conditions such as family circumstances and educational programmes on aspects of children's behaviour—all these are only a very few examples of the many different kinds of knowledge that psychologists working with children have generated. The list could be extended at length. The more we learn about the world of children and childhood the more we learn how little we know. But it is also important to note—and this is a point to which we shall return in Chapter 7—that few workers in these fields call themselves child psychologists. Nowadays our knowledge of child behaviour, as the Preface stressed, is gained from individuals who describe themselves as social psychologists, experimental psychologists, developmental psychologists, educational psychologists, and so on. But irrespective of the label under which the work is prosecuted, psychologists continue to advance our knowledge of the world of childhood.

(ii) *Predicting human development*

The desire for knowledge for its own sake is an important motive, but one which underpins activity in any academic field. It is hardly a sufficient reason to account for the explosive growth in the study of children's behaviour which has taken place in this century. Other reasons help to explain this phenomenon and it is to these that we now turn.

The second main reason why psychologists study children derives from the possibility of predicting the course of future growth. 'The child is father to the man' is a fairly common viewpoint. But psychologists have enabled the relationship to be charted with greater clarity and with greater precision. Piaget (1974) gives this as one of the reasons why the study of children will become of even greater importance to psychology as a whole. '... There is only one thing of which I am certain, and that is that developmental psychology, child development, will become more and more the central explanatory focus of all aspects of psychology. Adult psychology can only be a study of results. It is through child psychology and developmental psychology that we can study the mechanisms of formation and construction and thus find the explanatory level for all problems of general psychology.'

It is these questions of understanding and prediction which also motivate psychologists to study children. But in order to follow the way in which the child turns into the man, a long period of time is required. From birth to maturity in the human animal has been variously estimated as between 18 and 30 years, depending on one's view of the criteria of maturity. Indeed, some psychologists would argue that 'maturity' is a misleading concept. It falsely gives the impression that there is an age after which development ceases. Developmental psychologists think of development occurring across the life-span of an individual: it may proceed in many areas much more slowly after the late teens or early twenties, but it would be incorrect to think of an age at which change ceases. However we view this theoretically, the practical questions are the same. Prediction over long periods of time gives rise to many consequent problems—for example, research workers have to be employed over many expensive years; there are difficulties in tracing and following up individuals who move to distant places during the study. For these and other reasons, this kind of study, known in psychology as a longitudinal study, has not been mounted as frequently as might be the case. However, there is little doubt that those longitudinal studies which have been mounted have yielded findings of very great importance.

Perhaps the most interesting summary of the results of these long-term studies of human development has been given by Bloom (1964). Bloom argues that '... personality characteristics like intelligence, emotional attributes, etc., begin to stabilize from birth onwards, and even before the age of five can be shown to relate reasonably well to characteristics of the mature adult.' The size of the relationship depends on the characteristics being measured, and Bloom introduced the idea of 'half-life', the age at which half the variability of any characteristic in a group of adults can be predicted from a knowledge of the variability of that characteristic among the same persons as children. Some of these half-life data, which are *not* the same as ages at which 50 per cent of growth will have taken place, are given in the table below.

Table I *Estimates of "half-development" of selected characteristics, taking ages 18–20 years as criteria for full development*

Characteristic	Half-development age (in years)
	(adapted from Bloom, 1964, p. 205)
Height	$2\frac{1}{2}$
General intelligence	4
Aggressiveness in males	3
Dependency in females	4
Intellectuality in males and females	4
General school achievement	9

Like nearly all psychologists who have worked in the field of prediction, Bloom utters warnings against using early data to predict success in individuals, a point stressed, for example, by Clarke and Clarke (1972) in their review of prediction studies. There is a clear difference between predicting development of a group and predicting development of an individual. Bloom points out that '... a single early measure of general intelligence cannot be the basis for a long-term decision about the individual.'

Accurate prediction of later development is of course not possible without some knowledge of the experiences through which children will pass. There is a large and increasing body of research on the effect of different experiences and environmental influences on children's development. The kinds of experiences which any individual is likely to meet in life cannot, perhaps fortunately, be predicted. Consequently, to think that we will eventually be able accurately to predict the characteristics of the adult from a knowledge of the characteristics of the child is to seek the philosopher's stone.

But decisions have to be taken in the course of children's development, decisions which have considerable impact on a child's future life. The greater our knowledge of a child's likely development, the greater our knowledge of the effect of certain environments on development, the better the decisions that we take. This applies whether we are parents choosing a nursery school, teachers advising over syllabus choice, or careers officers concerned with a choice of vocation. For these reasons, knowledge of future development, even though it is based on foundations which are far from certain, is helpful. Some idea of future development is better than none at all. And it is largely on this basis that longitudinal studies are helpful to applied psychologists working with children.

In the early years of this century, psychologists were concerned to examine the development of broad characteristics like intelligence. One of the best known studies in this area is that of Lewis Terman, who began in 1921 to collect information on the intellectual development of a group of very able Californian school-children (Terman, 1959–60). The early work charted their school and college development and showed the relationship between childhood precocity and later scholastic success. Later study of the group was aimed at revealing details of the careers, the marriages, the attitudes and interests of the original group. While the original emphasis on the relationship between high ability, as measured by an intelligence test at an early age, and school and college performance has shifted, the method employed, regular study of the development of a group of children over a period of time—in this case most of the lifespan— has been consistent.

Later investigators have examined other, more specific relationships and there is a very clear sense in which the kind of quality studied in the major longitudinal studies has reflected the changing interests of psychological work with children. The Terman investigation was followed in the 1930s by other investigations, the most important of which focused on the intellectual development of a cross-section of children, not just an intellectual élite, as in the Terman study (e.g. Bayley, 1949; Honzik et al., 1948). They also began their studies with very young children, in some cases from birth, and so were able to provide information on the relative efficiency of the prediction of future intellectual development from different ages.

Other studies reflected a swing of interest from intellectual behaviour to affective behaviour, or behaviour characteristic of feelings and relationships. In the study conducted by the Fels Research Institute, USA, for example, Kagan and Moss (1962) reported data on the relative stability of qualities such as aggression, affection, and so on across the period from just after birth to the end of adolescence. Again it is possible to define the extent to which characteristics persist in groups and it is data such as these which provide the basis for much of Bloom's work, to which reference has been made.

More recently in Britain, the National Child Development Study has examined the development of a wide range of intellectual, emotional and physical characteristics of children, generating a number of publications (e.g. Davie *et al.*, 1972). The investigations have accumulated a vast body of data which enables relationships between particular attributes of the sample (or sub-samples) at a specific age to be related to the development of the same or other attributes at later ages. Psychologists have joined sociologists, doctors and others in multidisciplinary teams to collect data which predict development in many different ways. Some of these cross-disciplinary findings have been puzzling and raise many questions. For example, the extent to which smoking on the part of mothers relates to later physical and intellectual development of their children should provoke much further research, both medical and psychological. But a single instance can hardly do justice to the rich store of data on the development of children and adolescents which psychological research has now accumulated.

There are of course problems in data of these sorts. One obvious difficulty is that the data are themselves dated. It is easy—and entirely valid—to argue that data which show the relationship between intellectual development at two and scholastic attainment at 18 are inappropriate, since the intellectual experiences of two-year-olds today are very different from those of the two-year-olds of the study. Allowing for publication delays, the data would have been gathered some 20 years ago and child-rearing fashions, standards of living—qualities such as these, which may relate to the intellectual experiences of two-year-olds—change markedly over two decades or so.

(iii) *Influencing development*

This point raises the next question. What is it in the child's experience which determines the relationships which developmental enquiries such as longitudinal studies reveal? This leads to the third main reason why psychologists study children, for the answer to that question enables psychologists to play some part in influencing and affecting the development of children. All new knowledge leads the researcher and others to study the value it will have for application. This is as true of new knowledge in child psychology as it is of new knowledge in physics or any other science.

Perhaps the great contributions to knowledge made by child psychology can be ascribed to the introduction of a scientific approach, based on measurement. Thus everyone has known for centuries that a good home helps children's development. But it was not until the use of techniques for measuring child development and for measuring environmental qualities were developed by psychologists that the extent of the advantages given by different homes could be assessed.

It is worth noting that research results with clear consequences for practice often take a long time to gain application. Thus it has been said that it takes thirty years or more for the findings of educational research to infiltrate the schools. Similarly, findings from the scientific study of child development often take many years before they infiltrate the work of applied psychologists. One reason for this is ethical. It is easy for a scientist to conduct experiments intended to assess the application of a research finding to a manufacturing process. But it is a very different matter for a child psychologist to apply a research finding to a practical question relating to children. It may be clear from longitudinal studies that smoking in mothers bears a relationship to limited intellectual development in children. This does not however, mean that the smoking causes the intellectual stunting—other factors may be responsible for both the incidence of smoking and the limited intellectual growth. The causality of the relationship can only be tested by an experiment in which the smoking incidence is varied in a controlled way in order to examine the consequent variation in the intellectual growth of the children concerned. And while it may be experimentally good practice to test the effect in both directions, is it ethically justifiable to try to persuade mothers to increase their smoking in pregnancy in order to establish whether their children are, as a result, more damaged intellectually?

For reasons such as these, many experiments which would be permissible in the natural sciences are not permissible in child psychology. To some extent work with animals has been helpful, but this raises the hazardous problem of generalising from animal behaviour to human behaviour. Child psychologists have largely preferred to proceed slowly, gradually accumulating evidence from enquiries which are suggestive, rather than conclusive. Adults may volunteer for experiments; children may need protection from them.

The problem of the effect of background on development has been mentioned and will be discussed again in Chapter 4. But it is not until the accumulating evidence from major studies such as those of Douglas (1966), Fraser (1959), Wiseman (1964), and the National Child Development Study (Davie *et al.*, 1972) has been added to that of several Government Reports commissioned by the Ministry of Education and the Department of Education and Science (reviewed by McKinnon, 1976) that the extent to which different kinds of home background affect different aspects of scholastic development can be soundly evaluated. The assessment of the relationship between home background and development leads educationists to consider how this knowledge can be applied. Which part of the complex web of circumstances which makes up a rather crude environmental term 'home background' is most responsible for this difference in development? Is it the relationships which exist in the home? Is it the interest which the parents show in their children's efforts? Does the area or locality in which children live make a major difference to the way they develop? Much research in recent years has covered this particular question.

There now seems little doubt that one of the more important factors is the language which parents use to communicate with their children. The importance of language has been shown by many studies in the United States (e.g. Deutsch, 1965) and Britain (e.g. Cox, in press). The findings emerging from studies such as these lead to the development of language intervention programmes designed to help children from less advantaged homes to acquire the language through which the intellectual exchange of the worlds of school and work proceeds.

Not only is the kind of influence or intervention important, the optimum age at which it should be made available is equally critical. Bronfenbrenner (1974) has analysed data from many compensatory education programmes, aimed at compensating children for deprived backgrounds through enriched education, in order to shed light on their questions. He points to the value of intensive programmes, involving parents, and mounted early in the child's life (e.g. Heber and Garber, 1975).

Examples of this kind, showing how findings which arise from the study of children can be applied in order to influence major institutions of our society, such as the education system, or the system of child care, illustrate why people wish to study children. But all the examples given so far are examples of what one might term macro-influences. They relate to changing the major institutions of society in order to help the development of children *en masse* and in the long term. There are also the questions of how best to manage those contingencies in which individual children are involved and where adults, whether parents or those professionally concerned with children, may have to take quick action. How teachers manage individual children's behaviour in the classroom is an obvious example of this, but the management of children's behaviour involves many other individuals in society, such as social workers, youth leaders and, not least, parents.

The applied psychologist who works with children is aware of the effects of macro-influences on the mass of ordinary children. Indeed, one of the strengths of the psychologist's contribution lies in his knowledge of normal child development, the stages through which normal children pass and their characteristic needs. But many applied psychologists feel that their services are usually required for children whose parents and others are worried over unusual or abnormal development. Thus C. J. Phillips (1971) defined the central core of the educational psychologist's work as 'the identification, diagnosis and treatment of individual children with learning disabilities'. As we shall see later, not all psychologists would agree with the approach implied by the three words identification, diagnosis and treatment. It represents a medical model of the psychologist's work, a model which a proportion of applied psychologists reject. But there is little doubt that it is with individual children whose behaviour causes concern that most applied child psychologists work, and indeed this is one of the main assumptions on which this book is written.

It would be misleading to suggest that the application of research findings to those behavioural questions which child psychologists face is straightforward. There are differing theoretical approaches to the study of psychology which it would be inappropriate to examine in detail at this point. But it is important to realise that different approaches sustain different bodies of knowledge, supported by different lines of enquiry. Thus the management of children's behaviour can be based on the research findings of psychologists who follow the behaviourist tradition, believing that behaviour is acquired as a result of rewards, by way of a conditioning process, or on the research findings of psychologists who believe that behaviour stems from the individual's concept of self—or indeed from research based on other theoretical models. This is not the point at which to examine the pros and cons of the various approaches. The purpose of this paragraph is to indicate that the findings of research into the development of children lead psychologists to apply a number of different approaches to handling the problems of childhood, both those which exist on a macro-level and those which exist at the level of individual children. Some of the main approaches are considered in the next chapter.

| # How children are studied

Psychology, like every branch of science, may avail itself of two main methods of investigation: the method of experiment and the method of observation. Its recent advances have been due almost entirely to the former—the method of experiment. It is to that method that we owe the valuable conception of mental tests. Yet, in spite of the progress made in this and other directions, I am convinced that the second method—the method of observation—though neglected in recent years, will prove equally rich and fruitful.

From *The Backward Child* by Cyril Burt (third edition, 1950)

In the first chapter, Darwin's study of an infant was mentioned. In this, said to be the first scientific investigation of child development, the data which Darwin reports were gained, as he himself said, through regular observation of his child's development. Darwin does not tell us how frequently he observed the child. He does tell us that he recorded his observations in a diary at the time the phenomena occurred. Interestingly enough, he did not publish his material until some 37 years after he recorded it; one reason why it is important to record observations when they occur becomes quite clear. Had he not recorded observations at that time, the likelihood of him having had any trustworthy memory of those events some 37 years later would have been remote. The ways in which our memory of events is distorted by the lapse of time is studied in other branches of psychology. But the message of the findings applies as much to psychologists themselves as to others: it is essential for observations to be recorded as soon as possible.

The observations need not be written down. Some studies of children use machine recordings, perhaps to measure physiological data such as pulse rates. Other studies record children's behaviour on videotape or

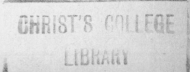

audiotape, so permitting later analysis at leisure. But all reputable studies, whatever the method of recording, record immediately.

Although Darwin is often cited as a pioneer of the scientific study of child behaviour, the literature concerned with the physical growth of children reports an earlier investigation, the work of a Frenchman, de Montbeillard. Between 1759 and 1777 he carried out a study of the growth of his own son by measuring his height at regular intervals from birth to eighteen years of age. The resulting growth curve (Figure 1, below) has become a classic in its field.

Figure 1 *The growth of de Montbeillard's son* (from Tanner, 1961)

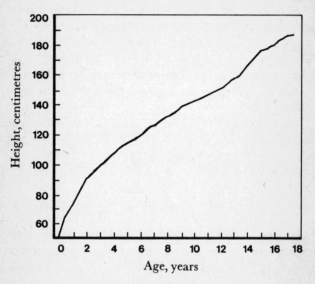

Note the rapid growth over the first two or three years, the steady but less marked growth across childhood, the spurt at adolescence (approximately thirteen to fifteen years, in this case) followed by a gradual cessation of growth. Like Darwin, de Montbeillard recorded his results when they were obtained. Unlike Darwin, he did not rely solely on his own observation of the phenomenon he was studying, but used a measuring instrument, in this case a centimetre rule. The instrument may have been simple; nevertheless it is an example of an increasingly widespread technique in psychological work with children—the use of 'instrumentation' to sharpen and extend human observation.

Not only have psychological studies of children relied more heavily on the use of measuring instruments. Some investigators, following in part the approach of the physical sciences, have attempted to carry out observations in controlled conditions. The reasons for this are similar to those which lie behind the use of instruments. The more carefully the environment is controlled, the less is the interference which may occur with the behaviour that is being studied and the more trustworthy will the observations be. The extract below, which is taken from the administration manual of an intelligence test published by Robert Gibson of Glasgow (Fleming, 1969), illustrates the attempt to control extraneous influences.

GENERAL DIRECTIONS

Before beginning the test see that each pupil is provided with a soft pencil or crayon. Have extra pencils ready in case of breakage. See that each pupil's name is written on his booklet.

Go through all preliminaries as quietly as possible—without excitement to the pupils. Try to suggest that this is a very nice new game that they are going to play.

Do not use the words "Test" or "Examination".

Say nothing about neatness.

After each practice test has been finished and the real test has begun, do not interfere with those who make mistakes of any kind

Use a watch with a seconds-hand for time-keeping.

See that the pupils stop promptly.

Follow directions verbatim. Do not attempt to memorise the instructions. Read them out, and keep carefully to the prescribed timing counting from the last word of the instructions to the beginning of the words "Pencils up" or "Pencils down".

Entrants to the Infant School should be tested in small groups of 10 to 15 pupils unless the examiner has assistants to help.

PROCEDURE

Distribute the booklets and tell the pupils not to open them, but to write their names on the cover and look at the pictures. While they are doing this, copy on the blackboard the three drawings on the cover. (In cases where the pupils cannot write, have the names written on the booklets before distribution.)

Say to the pupils—"We are going to play a new game with these books. I am sure you will like it. Hold up your pencils like this". (Demonstrate.) "Look at the pictures on the cover. There is a leaf, a foot, and a can just like these I have drawn on the blackboard. We are going to make marks on some of the pictures. I shall tell you just which ones you are to mark."

"First of all I want you to make a nice big mark right through the foot like this." (Draw a line through the foot on the blackboard.) "Do it, and then hold up your pencils again." (Move amongst them to be sure that each pupil is following the right method and making a distinct mark on the foot.) "That is very good. Now make a mark on the can." (Pause.) "Pencils up like this". (Move amongst them, and see that each child understands what is meant by making a mark.) "That is very good."

Test I.—"Now open your books like this (Demonstrate) so that you can see three cats. Hold up your pencils. Look at the three cats. Find the prettiest cat and make a mark on it." (While they are doing this, move amongst them to be sure that each pupil is making a visible mark on a cat.) "Pencils up. Now look at the three babies. Find the prettiest baby, and make a mark on it." (Time: 6 seconds.) "Pencils up. Now look at the three boats. Find the prettiest boat, and make a mark on it." (Time: 6 seconds.) "Pencils up."

"Now look over here, where you see three pence in the top row. Make a mark on the prettiest penny." (Time: 6 seconds.) "Pencils up. Now look at the three baskets in the next row. Mark the prettiest basket." (Time: 6 seconds.) "Pencils up. Look at the three tulips in the bottom row. Mark the prettiest tulip." (Time: 6 seconds.) "That was very good." . . .

And so on.

But other psychologists have followed different paths to gain data on children's behaviour. Although there are advantages in rigorously controlling the conditions in which measurement occurs, including that of isolating more clearly the behaviour being studied, paradoxically that very condition of isolation produces artificiality. Intelligent behaviour is not usually exhibited in real life under the conditions described in the extract above. For this reason some psychologists gather data on children by studying them in their natural surroundings: the classroom or the playgroup, for example. The essence of this approach, typified by H. F. Wright's study of children growing up in a mid-western town in the USA (Wright, 1967), is not only to study children's natural behaviour, but also to study the behaviour with as little intervention on the part of the observer as possible.

But this principle of avoiding intervention in order to study behaviour 'in the raw', as it were, is not appropriate for all purposes. When a doctor wishes to observe a child's physiological condition, he often plays a much more active role than that of a mere observer and the child is much more than a passive, neutral source of data. The doctor may prod the child, both physically and with words, seeking answers to questions. He follows up the child's answers with more questions, gradually accumulating more information. This idiosyncratic approach is the basis of the doctor's clinical examination and this 'clinical' technique has been applied by psychologists to the study of psychological qualities. Much of the data on which Piaget based his theories of the nature of child development were gained through the use of the *méthode clinique*, as illustrated by the following original Piagetian excerpt, taken by J. L. Phillips (1969) from Inhelder and Piaget (1958).

In this excerpt, Piaget is exploring the intellectual behaviour of a nine-year-old child, Bar through first asking Bar to classify a number of objects according to whether they will float or not. Bar's thinking is then tested through the following discussion.

Bar (nine years). [Class 1] Floating objects; ball, pieces of wood, corks, and an aluminum plate. [Class 2] Sinking objects: keys, metal weights, needles, stones, large block of wood, and a piece of wax. [Class 3] Objects that may either float or sink: covers. [Seeing] a needle at the bottom of the water [Bar] says:
'Ah! They are too heavy for the water, so the water can't carry them.'

'And the tokens?'

'I don't know; they are more likely to go under.'

'Why do these things float?' [Class 1]

'Because they are quite light.'

'And the covers?'

'They can go to the bottom because the water can come up over the top.'

'And why do these things sink?' [Class 2]

'Because they are heavy.',

'The big block of wood?'

'It will go under.'

'Why?'

'There is too much water for it to stay up.'

'And the needles?'

'They are lighter.'

'So?'

'If the wood were the same size as the needle, it would be lighter.'

'Put the candle in the water. Why does it stay up?'

'I don't know.'

'And the cover?'

'It's iron; that's not too heavy, and there is enough water to carry it.'

'And now? [It sinks.]

'That's because the water got inside.'

'And put the wooden block in.'

'Ah! Because it's wood that is wide enough not to sink.'

'If it were a cube?'

'I think that it would go under.'

'And if you push it under?'

'I think it would come back up.'

'And if you push this plate?' [aluminum]

'It would stay at the bottom.'

'Why?'

'Because the water weights on the plate.'

'Which is heavier, the plate or the wood?'

'The piece of wood.'

'Then why does the plate stay at the bottom?' . . . And so on.

These different approaches to collecting data are complementary, not competitive. Each has its advantages and disadvantages. Indeed, they are sometimes fused, as the development of 'Piagetian tests'

(Fogelman, 1970) indicates. With very few exceptions, irrespective of the approach followed, children are not antagonistic to the experience of being studied psychologically. Indeed, in most cases the experience, unlike some visits to the doctor or dentist, is actively enjoyable.

But although collecting data on children may be a pleasurable experience both for the children and the psychologist, there are still questions which need to be asked about the value of the data which the psychologist gains. One is the problem of generalising. Darwin made some interesting observations on the development of his own child: would those observations hold good for the range of children in the population at large? Would the child of a Liverpool seaman show the same characteristics, the same developmental stages as Darwin's son? Issues such as these can be illuminated by repeating enquiries and observations with a large group of children. If we are seeking to establish data on the development of the nation's children, then it is important that the group we establish (the sample) is reasonably representative of the nation's children (the population). Sampling theory, a branch of statistics, can help to make more confident generalisations, and data about the development of the nation's children could be built up by the use of any of the methods described above. The National Child Development Study, mentioned in Chapter 1, is an example of an attempt to establish data on the development of British children through assessing at regular intervals the characteristics of a sample which consisted of *all* children born in England, Scotland and Wales during a particular week in a particular year (3–9 March 1958).

Data which illustrate the range of behaviour in the child population are often of great interest. It is easy to forget the small range of child behaviour that any parent is likely to have met. Even a primary school teacher, closely acquainted with the behaviour of thirty or more different children each year, will, at the end of her career, have known well just over a thousand children. And the thousand children will probably not have been drawn from a wide range of geographical regions and family backgrounds. They would not have constituted a satisfactory sample for a psychological test—which can offer information about the characteristics of a child's behaviour set against a much richer background than that of a teacher with a lifetime's experience behind her. The illustration becomes much more pointed when the teacher is replaced by a parent, with close experience of two or three children only. Whether we like it or not, we are the prisoners of

our brief experience and the existence of data relating to the behaviour and development of large samples of children enables us to escape these limitations.

But other questions still remain. How would another observer have reacted to the situation which Darwin saw in his offspring? Would he have produced a set of observations which were similar or different? Some insight into questions such as these can be gained from studying the precautions which the observer follows to record his findings. A trustworthy observer scrupulously reports the care which he has taken to obtain his observations and the restrictions that he uses to limit his interpretations of them. This enables another investigator to repeat the enquiry, and thus either support or fail to confirm the results. The rigour with which the sources of information have been described affect incalculably the uses and the value of the results which the study gives us.

This search for rigour in investigation and for the ease of replication of results has led child psychologists to spend much effort and energy on their techniques of measurement. Observational checklists (see the example on pp. 54–5), methods for scoring children's drawings (e.g. Harris, 1963), diary record forms, are a very few examples of many techniques which have been devised in order to limit error due to the observer, not the child. But no matter how carefully the influence of the observer is controlled, as in the illustration on pp. 17–18, there will still be variation in the human characteristic being studied. No characteristic is completely stable: none permits us to make a single completely accurate measurement. Even an apparently stable physical characteristic like height will vary to some extent, depending on factors such as the time of day at which measurement occurs, the stance adopted, and so on. So for both these reasons, variation in the child as well as in the observer, psychological measuring instruments carry information about the trustworthiness or reliability of the data gained from them.

Characteristics of children can be measured with accuracy, but accuracy is not enough. A test of mathematics may be a very reliable measure, but it is unlikely to be a valid measure of probable success in, say, a career in journalism. For this purpose other measures, more relevant or more *valid*, are needed. So validity, the extent to which the test meets the purpose for which the psychologist uses it, is another important characteristic of measuring devices used to study children. And the title of the test is not always a satisfactory indication of validity. There are several measures marketed as tests of mathematics which are as much measures of children's ability to read the questions as they are of skill in handling mathematical operations.

The purpose of studying children may be to answer a specific question. For example, an investigator might be interested in finding out whether three-year-old girls use longer sentences in their speech than do three-year-old boys. Alternatively, and taking an example from the same field, an investigator may be interested in charting the way the length of children's sentences increases with age. If he is interested in a question of the latter sort, one which involves comparing the development of children of different ages on a particular characteristic, there are different approaches open to him. Thus he could, if he wished, take a group of children at birth and obtain a measure of their sentence lengths at different ages until they reach maturity. This is called a longitudinal study, of which de Montbeillard's work with a single child is an example. So is Darwin's study, even though the period of time did not extend from birth to maturity, but over a much shorter period. The essential feature is repeated assessment of a characteristic of children over a period of time. The results of a longitudinal study often enable a developmental curve to be drawn, like the one which appears in Figure 1.

There is, however, an alternative way of carrying out this kind of study. For example, the investigator who was interested in language development might well choose to establish 36 groups of children covering the eighteen six-month periods from birth to eighteen years of age. He could then measure the sentence length characteristic of each group and so plot a curve of development almost at once. There would, however, be several differences. Thus the time which the second investigator took would be very much less than the time taken by the first investigator. He might collect all his data in the space of a few weeks, as opposed to the eighteen years of the first kind of study. This is one of the very great advantages of what are called 'cross-sectional studies' as opposed to 'longitudinal studies'. There are other advantages, too. The short period of time means that one investigator can often carry out the whole investigation. Several of the major longitudinal studies of children's development, for example the Terman study (*Genetic Studies of Genius*) of the intellectual development and later careers of a group of intelligent children, reported in Chapter 1, required the services of several investigators over the many decades that the studies were running. Obviously economy is another great advantage. But these advantages are paid for in other ways. Thus the cross-sectional study very often masks great variations in the development of individuals.

J. M. Tanner (1961) in his now classical studies of children's physical growth has shown how the adolescent growth spurt, which is easily detectable in longitudinal studies, can be masked when groups of children, who enter the adolescent growth spurt at different times, have their own relative growth velocities smoothed when their data are merged with that of the group to which they belong. Davies and Williams (1975) illustrate this in relation to the growth of children's reading vocabularies, as the curves below indicate.

Figure 2 *The growth of word recognition skills*

(a) *A cross-sectional study*

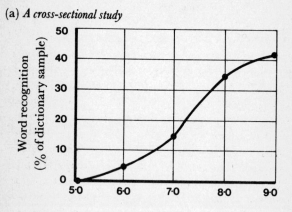

(b) *A longitudinal study, Case A*

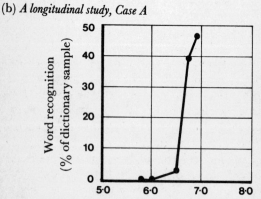

(c) *A longitudinal study, Case D*

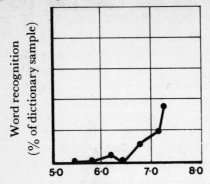

The curve in Fig. 2(a) is gained by a cross-sectional study. The curves of Figs. 2(b) and 2(c) are the result of the longitudinal study of individual children. The growth of early and late developers is masked in the cross-sectional study which smooths out rapid growth rates.

These two kinds of studies are examples of different approaches used to gain information about children's development. But, helpful though they may be over charting the growth of children's characteristics, they leave many questions still open. For example, one could well ask: 'What causes the growth spurt in children's reading vocabulary which Figures 2(b) and 2(c) show?' Studies may involve the use of controlled observation; they may involve specialised measurement devices; they might rely more heavily on the *méthode clinique*, but they do not necessarily allow us to make causal inferences or test hypotheses. They are descriptive, not explanatory. We may observe that the growth spurt in reading is paralleled by a change in school, for example. But we cannot draw the inference that the one is a consequence of, or a cause of, the other. In order to do this we need to design an experiment which allows us to intervene in development in controlled ways so that we can assess the result of our intervention and then, hopefully, make sounder inferences about the causal relationships between the experiences which children have had and their development. The central features of the experiments which psychologists set up lie in the control exercised by the experimenter over the experiences which the children receive. In ideal circumstances, one variable at a time is changed in the experimental situation, and given acceptable methods of assigning groups of children to different treatment conditions, safe inferences can be made.

The main disadvantage of the experimental approach is the achievement of controlled inference at the expense of reality. In the real-life situation, in the hurly-burly of the classroom, or school playground, or home situation, variables cannot easily be disentangled or separated from other events going on around them. Inferences we make from the experimental situation may not necessarily be very helpful in relation to the everyday world. In addition, there are ethical considerations which often prevent psychologists from carrying out many desirable experiments. Who would be willing to justify testing a new pedagogical technique on children over a period of four or five years, at the end of which one might satisfactorily demonstrate the technique to be of little value, having meanwhile damaged the life-chances of a group of children? Reasons such as these tend to push many child psychologists today back to the earlier approach of the controlled and more careful observation of the child in the real-life situation. The busy educational psychologist is very much more likely to use a mixture of focused observation on children's characteristics in school and at home allied to a version of the *méthode clinique* in work with children in the school psychological service. The experiment has a place, but it would be quite wrong to suggest that the greater scientific attraction of the experimental approach will lead, eventually, to the disappearance of less rigorous techniques from the armoury of the psychologist working with children.

Sometimes causal relationships are tested through less rigorous methods than the true experiment. For example, the effects of major environmental changes on the development of children in deprived or educational priority areas have been tested by survey work which could not be regarded as a well-controlled experiment (e.g. Halsey, 1972). Where controlled experiments are not possible, for reasons of realism, these other approaches must be followed.

One final point about these different approaches concerns the way in which they relate to each other. Anyone involved in work with children will recognise a situation in which an observation, perhaps made by chance, and perhaps made on one child, may lead to establishing a survey to test whether the observation is of more general validity. The data which the survey yields may in themselves generate ideas which can be tested by experiment and from which may well emerge yet newer ideas which will lead again to the cycle being followed as before.

These new ideas, which are themselves testable by further

observation and experiment, are usually cast in the form of hypotheses. The investigation of hypotheses through attempts to falsify or support them is an important part of the construction and modification of theory, a process which is as essential a part of child psychology as it is of other disciplines. But, as the preface indicates, it is not the intention of this book to discuss the principles of research and theory building in child development. Nevertheless, the process starts with the problems which strike those who work with children, and it is to these problems that we turn in the next chapter.

CHAPTER 3

Children's behaviour

When they put him in rompers the habits
Fanned out to close in, they were dressed
In primary colours and each of them
Carried a rattle and a hypodermic;
His parents said it was all for the best.

From 'The Habits' by Louis MacNeice

Chapter 1 indicated some of the problems of children's behaviour which were concerning parents some 400 or more years ago. Although many of these problems have a familiar ring today, nevertheless the situation is now much more complex. Thus Shakespeare's schoolboy creeping unwillingly to school may represent one of a number of different conditions. His unwilling behaviour is studied and categorized, and Rutter (1975), for example, distinguishes in this situation between truancy, fear of school, separation anxiety, social withdrawal and travel phobia, each of which has a characteristic behaviour pattern and demands a different treatment approach. The simple problems of earlier days have become much more differentiated and detailed. What are the kinds of problems and varieties of childhood behaviour which the psychological study of children has today identified?

In the late nineteenth century, Sully, a pioneer of child study, established a laboratory at University College, London, with the intention of offering advice on child development. Although this is correctly regarded as a milestone in the applied study of child behaviour, comparable to the theoretical importance of the publication of Darwin's paper, the main spur to the identification of problems of children's behaviour came from the education service. The introduction of the compulsory education Acts, as has been noted elsewhere, (e.g. Shepherd *et al.*, 1971) brought the teaching profession face to face with the behavioural difficulties of the child population. It was mentioned in chapter 1 that Warner, in 1890, crudely characterised children displaying behaviour difficulties as 'urchins who could not be taught and ruffians who could not be controlled'. This distinction between learning problems and personality problems is still the basis of the differentiation that is in use today. Not everyone would agree that this is the most useful of classifications, and indeed some would feel that it has led to an over-rigid and too deep separation of areas of behaviour which are inherently linked. Thus the basic Open University course in educational psychology, 'Personality and Learning', focuses on the relationships between these two areas.

The Warner quotation speaks of 'ruffians who could not be controlled', and is thus concerned with poor attitudes in terms of their effect on learning, not as damaging in their own right. This emphasis on failure to learn educational skills still tends to characterise the kinds of behaviour which teachers refer to school psychological services today. An example is taken from H. J. Wright (1974).

A CASE FOR INDIVIDUAL REMEDIAL TREATMENT

Reg was ten years old and a non-reader. He came from a good middle-class home, and had one sister a little younger. His ability was above average—on the WISC his verbal quotient was 108, and his performance quotient 106; he showed no visual perceptual or auditory weaknesses, and his motor control was good average. The only test findings that seemed significant were in the memory field. He was poor at remembering digits both forward and backward, and when given sentences from the Terman test again he performed badly. Both visual memory and auditory memory (Sibwell 3-letter word test) scores were at least three years behind his chronological age. His teacher said of Reg, 'I take ages to teach him something—he's got it, and then to my dismay within a few days he has forgotten it all.' He could not remember either the year or the month in which he was born, and he could name only five of the days of the week—nor did he know the months of the year. Christmas Day, he informed his examiner, was some time ago, but when exactly he could not remember. When first observed he failed to tell left from right in a number of short tests, and a year later was still unable to do so. Exploration of emotional difficulties did not reveal anything of significance. At school he enjoyed model-making sessions; he caused his teacher no disciplinary problems. It seemed therefore that Reg had a severe memory difficulty, and consequently could not assimilate enough basic knowledge on which to build further skills.

Wright describes Reg's behaviour as illustrating a group of children whose learning problems are linked to memory weaknesses and who need remedial treatment for this reason. Wright also offers other illustrations of the kinds of behaviour problems that teachers ask their educational psychologist colleagues to handle, not all of which are so clearly concerned with educational skills. These are:

   (i) a case of multiple handicap—a cerebral palsied child of eight, with severe speech and hearing difficulties whose headmistress was worried over his disruptive behaviour and lack of school progress;

  (ii) a hyperkinetic boy—a restless, physically uncontrolled five-year-old, who was failing to make the usual positive learning start;

 (iii) a slow learner—a girl of slow all-round development, unable to read or to handle number symbols at the age of transfer from infant to junior school;

 (iv) a severely educational subnormal five-year-old (who, on leaving a special school at sixteen was still unable to cope with the simplest of work situations);

  (v) a bright adolescent following an O-level course but failing to make progress;

 (vi) a highly intelligent seven-year-old asthmatic, who had great difficulty with reading and spelling and who was also very nervous.

These are examples of a few of the kinds of behaviour that concern schools sufficiently to lead them to call in the psychologist.

Can behaviour problems such as these be classified in any sensible way? Most educational psychologists work in the school psychological service, which was the first-established of the two main facilities that are available to deal with children's behaviour. The other is the child guidance clinic, traditionally run by a team of three specialists, of whom the educational psychologist is one. With a child psychiatrist usually in medical charge, the clinics receive many referrals from medical practitioners, in particular from family doctors. Consequently they deal with a range of problems which reflect children's home behaviour rather more extensively than do the referrals which are received by the school psychological service. Problems of sleeping behaviour and eating behaviour are understandably more frequently seen in child guidance clinics than in school psychological services. (Conversely, problems of reading difficulties and relationships with other children tend to be seen more frequently by psychologists working in the school psychological services.) The Underwood Committee, which was set up to report on the education of maladjusted children, and which reported in 1955, listed in an appendix a grouping of symptoms which were held to be indicative of maladjusted behaviour and which were used by child guidance clinics to classify children's behaviour problems. This list is given in Table II (from Ministry of Education, 1955).

Table II *A grouping of symptoms which may be indicative of maladjustment*

N.B. (i) This follows, except at a few points, the lines of a classification in use in child guidance clinics in this country [Britain].

(ii) For many of the symptoms listed, any and every manifestation does not indicate maladjustment, but only manifestations that are excessive or abnormal.

1 *Nervous disorders:*
  Fears—anxiety, phobias, timidity, over-sensitivity.
  Withdrawal—unsociability, solitariness.
  Depression—brooding, melancholy periods.
  Excitability—over-activity.
  Apathy—lethargy, unresponsiveness, no interests.
  Obsessions—rituals and compulsions.
  Hysterical fits, loss of memory.

2 *Habit disorders:*
  Speech—stammering, speech defects.
  Sleep—night terrors, sleep-walking or talking.
  Movement—twitching, rocking, head-banging, nail-biting.
  Feeding—food fads, nervous vomiting, indiscriminate eating.
  Excretion—incontinence of urine and faeces.
  Nervous pains and paralysis—headaches, deafness, etc.
  Physical symptoms—asthma and other allergic conditions.

3 *Behaviour disorders:*
   Unmanageableness—defiance, disobedience, refusal to go to school
   or work.
   Temper.
   Aggressiveness—bullying, destructiveness, cruelty.
   Jealous behaviour.
   Demands for attention.
   Stealing and begging.
   Lying and romancing.
   Truancy—wandering, staying out late.
   Sex difficulties—masturbation, sex play, homosexuality.

4 *Organic disorders:*
   Conditions following head injuries, encephalitis or cerebral tu-
   mours;
   epilepsy, chorea.

5 *Psychotic behaviour:*
   Hallucinations, delusions, extreme withdrawal, bizarre symptoms,
   violence.

6 *Educational and vocational difficulties:*
   Backwardness not accounted for by dullness.
   Dislikes connected with subjects or people.
   Unusual response to school discipline.
   Inability to concentrate.
   Inability to keep jobs.

7 *Unclassified.*

This classification illustrates some of the different kinds of behaviour
which causes concern to parents and teachers and which are not
specifically related to educational issues, which appear as only one of
the seven areas. A more objective approach to identifying the kinds of
behaviour which cause concern to parents was that of Shepherd *et al.*
(1971). They asked parents to complete questionnaires indicating the
extent to which children showed the behaviours listed in the left-hand
column of Table III. The extent to which children showed 'extreme
versions' of the behaviours is shown in the body of the table. This table
relates to children's behaviour at home, as assessed by parents. Note
that as far as parents are concerned only three of the items, 'dislike of
school', 'truanting' and 'reading difficulty' related definitely to the
school situation. Note also the concern that parents have over

Table III *Percentages of children recorded as showing 'extreme' types of behaviour at each age from five to fifteen*

GIRLS	5 years	6 years	7 years	8 years	9 years	10 years	11 years	12 years	13 years	14 years	15 years
Very destructive	2	—	1	—	*	*	—	*	—	1	—
Fear of animals	5	5	3	3	3	1	2	2	1	1	7
Fear of strangers	1	*	2	2	*	2	1	1	1	2	—
Fear of the dark	11	5	8	7	8	8	6	5	4	5	4
Lying	2	2	1	1	3	1	3	1	1	3	2
Dislike of school	1	3	2	4	3	2	3	3	5	7	4
Stealing	1	—	—	—	*	—	—	*	—	1	—
Irritability	10	9	9	10	12	10	12	10	11	16	11
Food fads	20	19	20	22	21	23	17	17	15	17	9
Fear of other children	—	*	1	1	*	1	*	1	*	1	—
Always hungry	5	6	6	10	9	10	10	13	15	11	16
Small appetite	21	17	21	18	13	12	12	8	7	8	5
Worrying	5	7	4	4	6	4	7	5	1	4	5
Whining	7	5	5	3	6	2	5	4	3	5	—
Restlessness	20	16	20	16	13	13	13	11	11	10	4
Underactivity	—	2	1	1	2	3	3	4	7	7	5
Jealousy	8	4	5	5	6	3	4	3	3	6	4
Wandering	*	*	—	1	1	*	1	2	1	2	4
Withdrawn	2	1	2	2	3	2	2	3	2	3	7
⌠Disobedient	10	10	8	8	11	7	10	10	12	14	14
⌡Always obeys	8	7	7	9	9	8	14	11	12	10	12
Truanting—at all	*	1	1	*	1	*	*	1	1	3	4
Tic	1	—	1	1	1	*	—	*	—	1	—
Mood change	5	2	4	3	5	3	5	5	7	7	14
Reading difficulty	5	7	14	14	10	13	10	11	5	7	4

BOYS	5 years	6 years	7 years	8 years	9 years	10 years	11 years	12 years	13 years	14 years	15 years
Very destructive	3	2	2	—	2	1	1	1	2	1	2
Fear of animals	3	3	2	1	1	2	2	1	1	1	—
Fear of strangers	2	1	1	1	—	*	*	1	2	*	4
Fear of the dark	9	6	8	8	10	7	6	5	2	2	2
Lying	5	3	5	2	3	3	3	5	4	2	2
Dislike of school	4	5	5	3	5	5	5	6	7	10	4
Stealing	—	1	1	1	1	*	1	1	2	1	—
Irritability	10	7	13	11	12	14	11	14	11	9	16
Food fads	19	20	22	22	22	18	23	19	17	17	16
Fear of other children	1	*	—	—	*	1	1	1	1	*	—
Always hungry	11	10	10	14	16	13	16	19	15	23	39
Small appetite	11	13	17	14	11	10	13	9	7	5	—
Worrying	4	5	5	7	6	5	3	3	5	4	5
Complaining	7	6	8	5	4	3	4	4	3	2	2
Restlessness	23	19	25	21	22	19	20	18	15	17	20
Underactivity	1	2	1	1	1	2	2	4	3	6	2
Jealousy	6	2	4	4	4	5	3	4	2	3	2
Wandering	3	1	2	3	3	3	3	4	4	8	2
Withdrawn	2	2	4	3	3	3	2	3	3	2	7
⌠Disobedient	17	11	14	12	12	13	13	14	11	12	9
⌡Always obeys	8	7	7	8	7	6	7	7	9	9	16
Truanting—at all	1	—	1	—	*	2	—	2	1	4	16
Tics	*	1	1	2	1	2	1	2	2	1	2
Mood changes	4	3	3	2	5	3	4	4	2	2	2
Reading difficulty	7	18	21	27	25	17	21	22	13	13	9

Note: * = less than 0·5 per cent.

behaviour like 'food fads', 'restlessness', 'small appetite', which feature quite prominently among children of all ages. The reader may be interested in the kinds of behaviour which seem to be prominent at particular ages.

One of the tendencies of recent work, as this study exemplifies, is to specify and delineate children's behaviour problems with greater precision. Thus Blackham and Silberman (1975) have described a very large number of problems which, on the basis of clinical work, they have found to concern both teachers and parents. They describe eighteen different kinds of school behaviour problems (by no means an attempt at a comprehensive listing) and summarise the work on each. These kinds of behaviours are, for example, inattention, forgetting assignments, profane language, out-of-seat behaviour, and so on. In the home situation they describe a wide group of behaviour problems, such as demanding behaviour, bedtime problems, failure to wear corrective devices, talking back, procrastinating before school, unfinished homework—in fact, the range of difficulties with which all parents will, at some time or another, have been concerned. For each behaviour they indicate ways through which the behaviour might be modified.

Unfortunately, this more careful specification and delineation of children's behaviour has not yet led to any broad agreement on a system of classification or taxonomy. The seven point classification of the Underwood report was based on practice followed in child guidance clinics. More recently attempts have been made to develop 'multiaxial' classifications of children's behaviour problems, which seems a sensible line of approach (e.g. Rutter et al., 1969).

In a similar vein, Herbert (1974) has used the statistical technique of factor analysis to provide a logical basis for classifying the ways in which teachers rate children's behaviour. He finds five factors, or 'axes of classification' (Table IV) of children's behaviour, whether good or bad.

Table III raises the question of incidence. How often does behaviour which causes concern occur? One of the classic longitudinal studies of children's learning and emotional behaviour is the National Child Development Study in which the development of a national sample of many thousands of children has been followed from birth to maturity. One of the more well-known findings is the observation that, at age seven, approximately one-sixth of all children have problems so

Table IV *Scheme for rating children's behaviour (after Herbert)*

Factor	Example of behaviour
A Personality problems, or introverted neuroticism	Easily flustered; depressed moods.
B Conduct problems or extroverted neuroticism	Aggressive behaviour; excitable.
C Competence	Good at class jobs; concentrates.
D Social extroversion towards adults	Seeks praise from adults; demands attention.
E Social extroversion towards children	Welcomes group work; popular.

marked that they need advice and guidance from other sources than the teacher or the parent.

The study which Rutter, Tizard and Whitmore (1970) conducted on the Isle of Wight is one of the best known cross-sectional investigations of the incidence of developmental problems in children. The results of that survey again showed that approximately one child in every six of those in the middle years of their schooling (that is between the ages of nine and eleven) were found to have a chronic or recurrent handicap. Handicap included intellectual retardation, educational backwardness, psychiatric disorder and physical hand-icap. About a quarter of these children had more than one handicap.

It will probably never be possible to identify with accuracy the numbers of children whose behaviour is seen as justifying recourse to psychological services. The very availability of those services will themselves affect the demand for them. And perceptions of what constitutes problem behaviour depends on attitudes of society at the time. Thus Whitehead and Williams (1976) suggest that whereas in the 1920s teachers were very concerned over children's sexual behaviour, today they regard sexual behaviour as of little consequence and are far more concerned over antisocial, aggressive behaviour.

There is therefore a sense in which it may be most productive to accept that incidence and needs are bound to vary. An acceptable rule-of-thumb estimate at present might take a minimum of one-sixth of the child population as in need of some assistance at any one time, but at the other extreme is the equally defensible view that the behaviour of

36 CHILDREN AND PSYCHOLOGISTS

all children might be screened psychologically on two or three occasions.

This last point relates to the way in which different behavioural problems vary with age. The diagram below, taken from Shepherd *et al.*, shows the way in which parents rated worried behaviour in their children over the ages from five to 15. The incidence will be seen to change markedly in relation to occasional worrying and carefree behaviour, but the incidence of children who often seem worried and indeed worry about many things remains fairly consistent at about five per cent.

Figure 3 *Variation in 'worrying' behaviour with age*

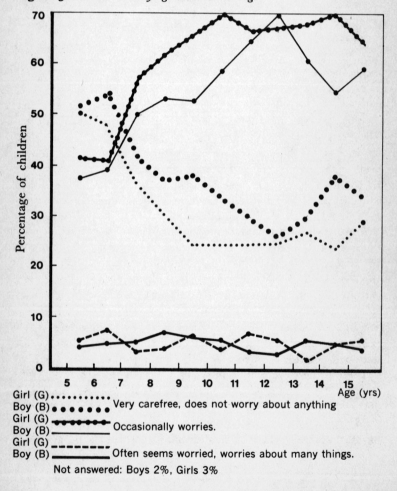

Girl (G) ••••••••••
Boy (B) ●●●●●● Very carefree, does not worry about anything
Girl (G) ●━●━●━●━
Boy (B) ●━●━●━●━ Occasionally worries.
Girl (G) ――――――――
Boy (B) ――――――― Often seems worried, worries about many things.
Not answered: Boys 2%, Girls 3%

Not only does the kind of behaviour which children show vary with age, it varies with the situation in which they find themselves. Many parents will be aware of the child who is a 'devil' at home but who is said by teachers to be an 'angel' at school—and indeed vice versa. Given a similar questionnaire on behaviour to complete, teachers rated the incidence of behaviour at each age range. Table V below, also taken from Shepherd *et al.*, indicates the way in which behaviour problems at school might or might not exist at home.

Table V *The relationship between the number of deviant behaviour items underlined by parents and the number of behaviour problems underlined by teachers*

Number of problems underlined by teachers		Number of deviant items underlined by parents							
		Boys				Girls			
		None	1–3	4–6	7–	None	1–3	4–6	7–
None	(No.)	740	846	108	35	817	847	135	47
	(%)	62%	55%	41%	43%	65%	61%	53%	45%
1	(No.)	259	387	62	20	283	308	68	29
	(%)	22%	25%	24%	24%	22%	22%	27%	28%
2	(No.)	115	158	43	10	107	127	24	13
	(%)	9%	10%	16%	12%	8%	9%	9%	12%
3 or more	(No.)	85	142	49	17	55	98	27	16
	(%)	7%	9%	19%	21%	4%	7%	11%	15%
Total	(No.)	1199	1533	262	82	1262	1380	254	105

Significance of association Chi-square = 73: 9 degrees of freedom: $P < 0.001$ Chi-square = 46: 9 degrees of freedom: $P < 0.001$

Thus 85 boys whose parents had identified no deviant items showed three or more problems when the teachers were asked to rate their behaviour. Conversely, 47 girls whose parents had indicated that they had seven or more items of deviant behaviour, showed (according to their teachers) no problems at school. To quote from the authors: 'nearly half the children whose parents' assessments put them in the most deviant group were apparently free from problems at school while more than one third of those who were without deviant behaviour at home had at least one problem recorded by their teachers.'

These illustrations give some idea of the kinds of behaviour which both parents and teachers find irritating in children and which they wish to see changed. But at the same time children themselves have their own views on the kinds of behaviour in others which upset them. This is another important field of enquiry. What parents and teachers may see as a dislike of going to school may in fact be related clearly and unambiguously in the child's mind with a specific dislike of the school toilets, or an inability to manage the school lunch situation, as Moore (1966) has demonstrated.

It is behaviours of the sort described in the preceding pages to which psychologists apply their skills of child study. Not all these behaviours are necessarily referred to the psychological services. Most workers make a very clear point of drawing attention to the low incidence of referrals (usually to child guidance clinics) in comparison with the relatively high incidence of similar behaviour among the population as a whole. Shepherd and his co-workers were particularly interested in this question. We have already seen that about a sixth of the children in the early years of schooling, according to their teachers and parents, could benefit from some help over their behaviour. Yet very few receive that kind of help. Thus Hyde (1975) reports that even in an inner-city depressed area in the USA, where the incidence of behaviour and learning problems is likely to be higher than the average (see Chazan, in press), only two per cent of the child population was referred to the school psychologists. The Summerfield Report (Department of Education and Science, 1968) showed the regional variations in treatment rates at child guidance clinics in England and Wales, where treatment rates in some regions were between two and three times those in others. Fig. 4 demonstrates this.

There are several reasons for variations such as these. Not only do perceptions of the role of the psychologist vary very much, but in some areas psychologists are very thin on the ground. It is this last point which is now beginning to change so much more rapidly. The much greater likelihood of teachers and parents coming into more frequent contact with psychologists working in their area means that perceptions, too, will change and referrals increase. The detailed description of problems of behaviour which psychologists and others have identified and described are likely to return to them as the questions of supportive parents and interested teachers wishing to discuss and seek help over the behaviour of the children with whom they are most closely concerned.

Figure 4 *Regional treatment rates at child guidance clinics, 1966*

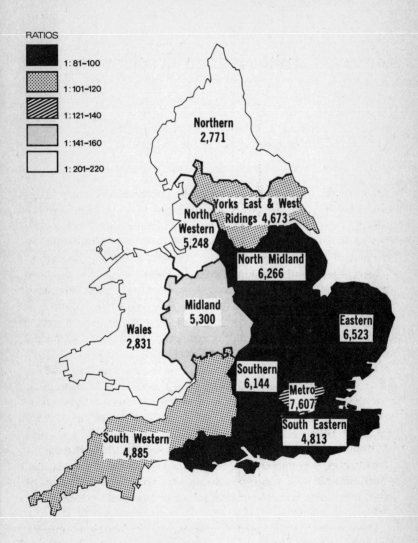

RATIOS

1 : 81–100
1 : 101–120
1 : 121–140
1 : 141–160
1 : 201–220

Northern 2,771

Yorks East & West Ridings 4,673

North Western 5,248

North Midland 6,266

Midland 5,300

Eastern 6,523

Wales 2,831

Southern 6,144

Metro 7,607

South Eastern 4,813

South Western 4,885

Total number of pupils treated in England and Wales during 1966 was 57,061 (ratio 1:131); regional totals are shown on the map. There are large local variations in ratios within some regions.

| Influences on development

Tout comprendre, c'est tout pardonner.

The more the psychologist knows of the circumstances which affect children's development the better equipped he is to deal with the behaviour that the last chapter discussed. Successful remedies usually depend on understanding causes, whether these lie in the individual or are part of the fabric of his society. Broadly speaking, the various influences which affect children's development are grouped into two main categories, hereditary and environmental. The hereditary influences are those carried by the genes, tiny components of the cells of which our bodies are constituted. The genetic pattern which a child carries is determined at conception, the genes being derived from the sperm of the father and the egg of the mother.

The environmental influences consist of all the experiences which affect the newly-formed individual from the moment of conception onwards. The first environment is of course a pre-natal environment within the mother, but by far the greater bulk of psychological work has until recently concerned itself with the effect of post-natal environments on children's development. Before discussing these kinds of influences, it is important to spend a short time on the lively and sometimes bitter controversy about the relative importance of hereditary influences as opposed to environmental influences on children's development.

There is little doubt that for some human characteristics, genetic factors are of major importance. An obvious example is height, All our evidence about the development of children's height suggests that the final mature height which a child attains depends almost entirely on the genetic pattern with which he is endowed, and apart from long periods of severe malnutrition, there are few environmental variations which are likely to produce marked changes in the mature height reached. However, some physical characteristics, such as hair colour, are clearly even less affected by the environmental experiences which a child enjoys—though even in that case it would be a brave individual who would take his stand on the absence of any environmental effect whatsoever. For example, the bleaching effect of the sun might be considered as one environmental effect making some difference to a quality as apparently stable as hair colour. But the results of most environmental effects on such characteristics are trivial.

The argument over the relative effect of hereditary and environmental qualities becomes much more intense when psychological characteristics are considered. The main work has been done on intelligent behaviour, usually measured by scores on intelligence tests. Much of the research has been based on studies of identical twins—that is, individuals with apparently identical genetic patterns. These are the twins of the novel, the brothers or sisters who cannot be told apart. Usually, identical twins are raised in similar home environments (that is, in their own family) and share similar educational experiences. So they have been raised in very similar environments as well as being similarly endowed. But occasionally, for various reasons, the members of a pair of identical twins will have been separated, and in these circumstances it is possible to examine the development of a pair of individuals who have apparently identical heredity, but who have experienced different environments. By repeating the enquiry on several pairs, estimates can be made of the effect of different environments on the development of specific characteristics. As might have been expected, environmental differences of the kinds studied have little or no effect on those physical characteristics such as height or hair colour. But by examining the variations in scores on intelligence tests, estimates of the much more interesting effect of a range of environments on intellectual development can be made.

It is the applicability of this technique to the study of development of psychological characteristics which has led to controversy. Perhaps the most detailed criticism is to be found in Kamin (1974), though many other writers have raised questions on the same point. The consensus of the findings of those workers who have nevertheless used this approach was that between two-thirds and four-fifths of the spread of intelligence test scores in the population could be ascribed to the influence of hereditary factors, while the remaining one-third to a fifth could be ascribed to environmental factors (e.g. Vernon, 1976). It must be noted however that Jencks (1972), who has carried out one of the most searching analyses of this problem, puts the heredity : environment estimate as 45 per cent : 35 per cent for the USA, the remaining 20 per cent of variation being accounted for in a different way.

Note that the 'two-thirds' figure mentioned above does not mean that for any one individual two-thirds of his intelligence is hereditary and one-third environmental. The statement applies to the spread of scores in the population. Its implication can be illustrated by considering the situation in which everyone grew up in identical environments. In that event there would still be a range of intellectual ability in the population. The range would, however, be narrowed to approximately two-thirds or so of its current range. The spread of scores would be due to hereditary factors alone.

Alternatively, if we could imagine a situation where everyone was endowed with identical heredity (a race of human clones), but was raised in a range of different environments, then the spread of ability in the population would be very much less and would in fact shorten to only about one-third of the existing spread. The effect of heredity in giving us individuals with different intellectual skills is said to be more influential than the effect of environment. But, as stated above, this kind of inference has been widely questioned for a variety of reasons by a number of biologists and psychologists.

No-one can seriously deny the influence of genetic factors on psychological development. For example, Down's Syndrome (formerly known as mongolism) is without doubt associated with restricted intellectual development and is equally doubtlessly caused by chromosomal abnormality in the individual. Similarly, no-one can deny the effects of environment on intellectual development. The so called 'attic children' (see for example, Clarke and Clarke, 1976), who have been kept in severely impoverished surroundings, are examples of children whose intellectual development has been severely restricted and where an improved environment can lead to remarkable intellectual gains. Neither side in the debate would question the importance of the influences supported by the other; the nub of the argument lies in the extent to which it is meaningful to try to quantify environmental effects on development. And the argument does have practical implications.

For example, a range of 'Headstart' programmes was instituted in the 1960s in the USA. These programmes were designed to improve the development of impoverished children, largely in the big American conurbations, by providing them with an enriched environment during the long summer holidays. The effects of the Headstart programmes were evaluated in a number of separate investigations, and the results, though debatable, were far from unequivocally favourable. The supporters of hereditary influences on intellectual development say that uncertain results of this sort are quite consistent with their position. They argue that the poor intellectual development shown by these children at school is due primarily to their inherited intellectual qualities and that improvements in the environment are unlikely to make a major difference to the children. The environmentalists, on the other hand, say that the best environment for improving the children's intellectual development has not yet been designed, and point to the marked success of a few of the Headstart programmes as indicating promising lines for future research and application. They are in a sense the successors of James and John Stuart Mill, whose views are quoted by Cavenagh (1931), as follows: ' "In psychology," says J. S. Mill of his father, "his fundamental doctrine was the formation of all human character by circumstances, through the universal Principle of Association, and the consequent unlimited possibility of improving the moral and intellectual condition of mankind by education." '

Many psychologists and others regard the question of the relative importance of heredity and environment as academic, in both senses of the word. Clarke and Clarke (1972), for instance, argue that it is far more productive to ask to what extent differences between individuals can be attributed to either influence, and immediately make the point that the answer will vary for different individuals. The paradox in the situation is best illustrated by considering what would happen if, by some means, we were able to design for each child the environment which was ideal for his development. All variation, whatever it might be (and it would not be the same as in the 'identical environment' situation described on p. 42) would then be linked to differences in heredity. So the more attention we pay to environment, the better the environment we produce, the more we increase the relative (but not the absolute) importance of heredity for human characteristics.

So the debate continues. But so far as the practising psychologist is concerned (that is, the psychologist who works with children presenting problems), it is with the environment that he must primarily be concerned. Although we now know that the cause of

Down's Syndrome lies in the child's genetic composition, a condition which cannot be altered, nevertheless the psychologist concerned with handicapped children is able to suggest a variety of ways in which environments can be improved and through which the competencies of Down's Syndrome children can be considerably increased. The diagnosis of a hereditary condition is, so far as the psychologist is concerned, irrelevant. His task is to design the learning experiences which increase and expand a child's opportunities to learn skills which will be useful in his immediate circle.

That this is possible has been amply demonstrated through the body of work being accomplished by the Hester Adrian Research Centre (Mittler, various dates). The idea applies not only to children who are severely handicapped: changing the environment so as to improve child development is an aim which is of relevance to children of all abilities and all characteristics. And the rest of this chapter examines the kind of environments which have been shown to be effective in children's successful development.

In order to examine the environmental influences which affect development, we shall concentrate on one aspect of development—the growth of cognitive qualities such as school attainment and intelligence, the aspect of child development which has stimulated more work and which has attracted more attention than any other. That situation may in itself be a comment on the relative values of a society which chooses to study the intellectual qualities of its children in preference to their moral or social qualities. The situation is changing, as Biggs's (1976a) recent review of work on the effect of school experiences on moral development shows. But for the purposes of this chapter the discussion will be limited to cognitive development.

In order to bring some order into the welter of findings, environmental influences will be classified into three broad groups: first, home influences; second, school influences; and third, other influences, including the impact of the peer culture and society generally. This division is one of convenience. In using it, it is important to remember that the different groups are necessarily interlinked. Until fairly recently at least it was likely that a child from a materially good home with sound family relationships would be going to a relatively well-equipped school which had succeeded in attracting to it better teachers. The local peer group and youth organisations would probably be stimulating, active bodies, and the three elements of the environment that we have identified would be influencing development in a similar direction. The converse would apply to a child living in a priority area. The chances of the home being poorer materially and psychologically would be greater; the school would probably be less well-equipped and staff turnover would be higher; delinquency among the child population would probably be greater. So although research techniques can isolate the effects of these different influences, nevertheless it is important to remember that in reality there are close associations among them and for individual children the various influences are usually cumulative and build on one another.

The effect of home on children's development has been a matter of common-sense observation for many years. But it is only in comparatively recent decades that psychologists have tried to measure the effect of various influences linked to the home. This step forward has depended on the construction of suitable measuring instruments; devices for assessing the quality of the home environment have multiplied markedly in recent years. The simple rating scales, on which homes were graded on perhaps a five-point scale depending on the observer's unverified opinion of the child's home, have now been supplanted by a variety of different techniques. For example, the Plowden Report (Department of Education and Science, 1967) which represents one of the landmarks in work in this area, assessed the literacy of the home in part through counting the number of books which the parents possessed. This is a crude but not unsatisfactory index. The quantity and quality of the newspapers and magazines taken have also been used for assessing another aspect of the literacy of the home and considerable ingenuity has been shown by research workers in this field.

It has always been easier to measure the material attributes of children's homes than to measure abstract qualities such as literacy. The presence of amenities such as washing machines, television sets, and so on; the adequacy of the parental income; the ratio of inhabitants to the household floor space—all these have been used as indices of the home's material qualities, and then related to measurements of children's intellectual development.

A third aspect of the home environment has perhaps been the most difficult of all to measure. This is the quality of the relationships existing within the family. There are penetrating psychological devices for assessing this, but these are usually lengthy and time-consuming and involve employing highly-trained clinical personnel.

For research purposes this would usually be too expensive a method of proceeding. So simple objective techniques have been used to assess the psychological stability and coherence of a family unit. Sometimes these are as crude as recording whether the family is a 'one-parent' family or not. Usually they are less unsophisticated and may involve interviews with family members. Thus in the Swansea Compensatory Education Project, aimed at studying the development of deprived children, the relationships within the family, were assessed through an interview with a social worker.

Most of the British investigations concerned with home influences on development (e.g. Department of Education and Science, 1967) demonstrate the relative importance of psychological influences such as family stability and the presence of a stimulating environment in comparison to the material qualities of the home. (For a summary of the major investigations see McKinnon, 1976.) In a sense this is a finding which would not be unexpected. The child who comes from a well-off home in the material sense, who is surrounded by the trappings of luxury, will nevertheless not be likely to respond to school unless he has the interest and encouragement of a stable family. Wealth is not a precondition for interest, encouragement and stability—these qualities can readily be found in the impoverished section of the community as well as among the well-to-do. This is not to deny the effect of severe poverty on children's development. The strains that severe poverty causes are enough to damage the development of any child. But in much of our society, provided parents are reasonably satisfied with the level of their income (not its absolute level, but its level in relation to their needs), there seems little doubt that the quality of the material environment has no great effect on children's school progress and intellectual development.

The school itself is the second main environmental infuence on children's development. A stimulating, encouraging school with interested teachers and a lively, active life, can make a marked difference to a child's intellectual development. Schools vary also in their material characteristics, their equipment, their setting, their buildings, and so on. Some psychologists have developed 'amenity indices' for measuring these aspects of the school environment (Laing, 1971). Again, relating qualities such as these to children's development shows how uninfluential they are in comparison with the less tangible qualities of spirit and purpose—what it is now unfashionable to call 'tone.' It is interesting that, as with home influences, the psychological is more important than the physical.

Those investigations which have sought to separate the influence of the school from the influence of the home (e.g. Department of Education and Science, 1967) find that the school influences are the less important. To quote Peaker (1967), writing in the Plowden Report, (slightly paraphrased):

> The variation in parental attitudes can account for more of the variation in children's school achievement than the variation in home circumstances, which in turn accounts for more than the variation in schools.

That is an important starting point for the psychologist who is investigating learning problems in primary school children.

The third group of influences—that is, the effect of the peer group, the media and so on on children's intellectual and cognitive development—has been less studied. The effect of these influences on other characteristics, such as children's values and attitudes, is widely known and has been quite heavily investigated. For example, the attitudes of adolescents to many issues are often more closely related to the attitudes of their peers than to those of their parents. Although there are many studies which draw relationships between 'isolation' from group friendship patterns and poor attainment, many of these have been set in the context of identifying children with learning or behaviour problems. There is as yet no body of work on the contributions of peer-group membership to school performance which can stand comparison with that concerned with the effects of home and school. The same point applies to studies of the effects of the media. We need studies to extend the work of Ball and Bogatz (1970), which was concerned with the effects of exposure to one specially constructed series of programmes—*Sesame Street*—on aspects of children's cognitive development.

How effective are these influences on children's development? One point to reiterate is that effectiveness depends very much on the age of the child. The younger the child, the more potent are home influences. Thus for children entering school for the first time the variation in development which is ascribable to the environment will have been largely generated by the home, less by society, and not at all by school. On the other hand, the older the child, the greater the attachment to school, the greater the experience of school and the less influential will be parents and the home situation.

Various investigations have attempted to examine the relative influence of home, school and other factors on the intellectual development of children at different ages, usually in relation to their scores on standardised tests of reading and arithmetic. This has usually been done by separating out the extent to which the spread of scores can be associated with differences in homes or in schools, and so on. In more technical terms, the variance is partitioned. This leads to conclusions such as that quoted from Peaker, above. Although this approach is useful, there are two important considerations to bear in mind.

We saw with the heredity-environment debate that both these qualities are essential to a child's development. The same point applies to home, school and other influences. No child can develop satisfactorily in our society without that development being influenced by his home, by his school and by the experiences he gains outside both home and school. When policy decisions on major social and educational spending are made it may be very important to have some measure of the relative effects on children of, say, mother's attitude as opposed to the size of a class. This may affect a decision on whether to expand the training of social workers or teachers. However, the practising psychologist is usually first concerned with individuals, and secondly with policies (though see Chapter 6, p. 66). He will need to explore all influences on the child, not just that set which research has shown to be the most important. This leads to the second point. Research findings are valuable, but research findings usually relate to large groups of children. It is because children within the groups vary, it is because the findings of research are not necessarily applicable to individual members of the group in which the research was carried out, that it is essential for the psychologist to carry out an individual study of each child who is referred to him. He can identify the extent to which, for example, parents' attitudes to a child are unusually over-protective, or rejecting—and often parents are themselves surprised to learn how much their own behaviour to their children differs from that of other parents. He can also identify the extent to which a child is part of a school community or isolated within it. But the pattern of influences on any child is unique. Research findings help to direct the psychologist's search for explanations: they do not determine his findings. The importance of the individual study to applied child psychologists cannot be over-emphasised, and the way in which this is carried out is one of the themes of the next chapter.

CHAPTER 5

Working with children, 1

I was much too far out all my life
And not waving but drowning.
From 'Not Waving but Drowning' by Stevie Smith

As the first chapter indicated, psychologists study children for different, but linked, reasons. Not only do psychologists study children to understand and predict child development, they also work with children in order to apply that knowledge to help the development of children, both normal children and children with problems. These two kinds of reasons, research and its application, are interlinked, because the applied field depends very much on the research field for the knowledge on which its practice is based. Similarly, the research field depends in no small measure on the applied field for the identification of some of the issues which it investigates. The principles and methods of psychological research are not the main concern of this text, however. Readers with interests in research can consult specialist texts (e.g. Kerlinger, 1973; Mussen, 1960). In this chapter we concentrate on outlining some of the ways in which applied psychologists work with children who are referred to them.

With which children do applied psychologists work? This very question is one which many present-day psychologists would like to see rephrased. 'With which kinds of child behaviour do psychologists work?' would for many applied psychologists be a more appropriate question. Whether a psychologist works with an individual child or works with child behaviour is an issue which raises metaphysical as well as methodological questions. The last chapter, which outlined the kinds of problems with which child psychologists deal, ignored this issue in order to avoid complicating the discussion. But there is a very real difference between the two standpoints, in particular where their implications for treatment are concerned, and on p. 59 we return to this point when different treatment approaches are discussed. For the time being we shall use the more common and perhaps more intelligible phraseology of the first question.

The last chapter mentioned the view that all children should be seen by a psychologist at some stage of their development and preferably at an early stage. There are those who argue that the routine medical checks on children's physical growth should be paralleled by routine psychological checks on their behavioural development. At present a child is usually seen by applied psychologists only when someone is sufficiently concerned about behaviour to refer the child to a psychologist. Of course, children's behaviour and development are being monitored in any case, and monitored very regularly. But the main monitors are the parents. And while parents are in many cases very perceptive and skilled observers of their children, at the same time they do not possess the applied psychologist's knowledge of the wide range of child behaviour, nor his expertise in dealing with it.

The advantages of routine psychological screening are fairly clear. Inappropriate and damaging behaviour patterns which parents and children were either accepting or ignoring could be modified. Developmental abnormalities could be identified, in many cases years before they came to light in the normal course of events, and suitable help given. Preventive measures of various kinds could be instituted early. The case of the severely subnormal boy, mentioned on p. 30, is an illustration of a child whose developmental problems were picked up by the experienced eyes of his teacher when he first entered school. But much in the way of special learning programmes and preparation for school could have been instituted earlier had this lad's slow development been identified then— as it could have been—through a psychological check on his development. Much unhappiness might have been avoided.

Should routine checks of child development be carried out by psychologists, or by parents, or teachers, or others who come in regular and close contact with every child? This question we take up in the next chapter. At present psychological checks on child development are, with few exceptions, carried out by psychologists on those children whose behaviour has led to a referral to them—a situation which may well change as practice alters.

Who are the individuals who refer children to psychologists? The person who is in contact with the child throughout the whole of his

development, from birth to maturity, is of course the parent. B
parents have not always been aware of the availability of psychologists, nor of the kinds of services they offer. So although parents are
increasingly seeking psychological help over their child's development,
most referrals to psychological services come from professional
colleagues who are usually better informed about psychological advice
than most parents.

During a child's early years, when his mother is in fairly close touch
with the community health services and possibly the hospital services,
it is through personnel such as doctors, health visitors, physiotherapists
and others, that contact is made with the psychological services. Some
readers may wonder what kind of psychological problem the mother of
a young pre-school child may possibly have. But the difficulties can be
manifold. Parents are concerned over every aspect of their child's
development. They are eager to know whether their child's speech is
progressing as it should be; they are eager to know whether their
child's motor milestones, his crawling, his standing, his walking, are in
accord with expectations; they want to know whether his reasoning
powers are going to stand him in good stead later on; they wish to be
reassured that the aggressive or withdrawn behaviour that their child
may occasionally show is not unexpected at his age, and will not lead to
problems in the future. The questions are endless. There are many
colleagues with particular specialist knowledge of some kind in this
field—developmental pediatricians, child psychiatrists, social workers,
for example. But the applied psychologist is the scientist who claims to
have had a training which concentrates on the development of
children's behaviour, both normal and abnormal, and many parents of
young children who have quite naturally consulted their general
practitioner over the behaviour of their young child have found that
he has suggested seeing the psychologist.

During the school years, children are in close contact with teachers
and so it is not surprising that the schools have in the past been the most
prolific source of referrals to psychologists. Nevertheless other services
make frequent contact, primarily but not solely for the purpose of
gaining psychological advice on children. The most recent analysis of
these contacts still seems to be that given in the Summerfield report
(Department of Education and Science, 1968) which illustrated the
relative frequency of contact between educational psychologists and
other services in the diagram (slightly modified) given below.

Figure 5 *Frequency of contact between educational psychologists and other services*

■ Frequent contact   ▨ Less frequent contact   □ Little or no contact

(a) Services specified in questionnaire: 330 respondents

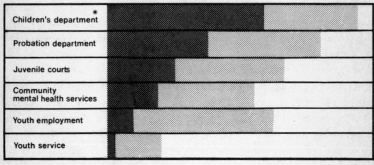

Children's department *

Probation department

Juvenile courts

Community mental health services

Youth employment

Youth service

* Now part of Department of Social Service

(b) Services other than those specified in questionnaire: on same scale information volunteered

School health service

Health visitors maternity services etc

Health dept. training centres

Hospitals inc. psychiatric units

General practitioners

Hearing and speech therapists/units

Educational welfare officers

Approved schools Remand homes

Police inc. J.L.Os

No contact

Most of the health functions mentioned are now incorporated in the Area Health Authorities.

In what ways do applied psychologists work with th
referred by these services and the behaviours they present?

Perhaps the very first issue which faces the psychologis
telephone rings and a problem is referred, is to decide whether his
psychological skills are necessarily the best to cope with the problem.
Although some problems, such as lack of concentration, or poor
reading, for example, clearly fall within the range of behaviour with
which the psychologist deals, they may nevertheless be the results of
medical conditions which must be handled by a doctor. Similarly, a
number of behavioural difficulties can be much better handled by the
range of skills offered by social workers and the social services. So the
first task is to decide whether the problem has come to the right person,
and to answer this question information is required—behaviour must
be studied.

Information comes in the first place from the person who refers the
child. But since one of the questions that the psychologist will want to
ask relates to the consistency of the behaviour (that is, whether it is
displayed in a variety of different situations), it is fairly important for
him to seek information from individuals who know the child in
different contexts—obviously the parent, possibly the teacher, possibly
the youth worker, perhaps a social worker, and so on. Not only is it
important for him to establish how consistently the behaviour is
displayed: he will also need to know when in a child's life has the
behaviour or behaviour like it been displayed previously and to what
extent—whether it originated after a change of school, or the birth of a
brother or sister, for example. At this stage of the investigations it is
unlikely that very precise information about the extent and history of
the behaviour is required; more of an idea or a rough assessment of the
size of the problem is being sought. Often, of course, this preliminary
investigation may disclose that the problem is minimal—the parent
worried about her child's bed-wetting may turn out to be the mother of
a five-year-old whose child wets the bed once a month. Alternatively,
further enquiries may have the opposite effect, disclosing the existence
of other problems about which the original referrer may not have
known. A teacher's concern about a child's poor reading may in turn
reveal that the child is also getting on very badly with his mother and
may be pilfering from neighbours. This is a problem of a different
order of dimension and will need different kinds of procedures. In
other words, the initial enquiries give the psychologist some kind of feel
for the problem which enables him to decide his next step.

In all these situations the need to consult with parents and other colleagues has been mentioned. But others involved with the child will not always know that he has been referred to the psychologist. It is rare and indeed unforgiveable for a parent not to be so informed, but some parents will refer a child to a psychologist without the school knowing, and indeed sometimes asking that the school is not informed. It is at this point that ethical dilemmas occasionally arise when assumptions over confidentiality may be in direct conflict with a child's welfare—a situation which is not confined to psychologists, of course.

The information which the psychologist obtains may be gained through discussions or sometimes by asking colleagues or parents to complete a more structured observation schedule which enables the child's behaviour to be specified more precisely than in an unstructured discussion. An example of a section of a schedule which is sometimes used to gain information on a child's behaviour is illustrated below (Figure 6).

Figure 6 *A section of a children's behaviour questionnaire* from Shepherd, M., Oppenheim, B. and Mitchell, S. (1971)

C. BEHAVIOUR AND HEALTH PROBLEMS

1. *Please underline,* in the list below, any items which describe this child as he often is:

(a) Very restless, can't sit still for a moment
(b) Cries more than most children
(c) Has a stammer
(d) Has other speech difficulty
(e) Often tells lies
(f) Has stolen things on one or more occasions
(g) Is very easily frightened
(h) Bites finger nails
(i) Sucks thumb or finger
(j) Very irritable, easily becomes cross or annoyed
(k) Has had one or more temper tantrums at school during this year
(l) Is unco-operative in class
(m) Very shy, finds it difficult to mix with other children
(n) Has wet or soiled self at school during last year
(o) Has noticeable twitch of face or body
(p) Worries more than other children

(q) Aggressive towards other children
(r) Very quiet or withdrawn
(s) Very moody—on top of world one minute, down the next
(t) Not interested in school work
(u) Has on one or more occasions during this school year shown fear of school—that is, tears on arrival or refusal to come into the building.

2. Has this child, to the best of your knowledge, any medical disability or chronic illness? (Please do *not* ask the child.) If so, what is it? Does it affect performance or participation in school activities? . . . .
. . . .
. . . .

(This schedule is part of a larger questionnaire for teachers.)

Sometimes a fairly detailed history of a child's development is required, including information about his circumstances and family, as well as about events which took place many years beforehand. An example of the kind of detail which may be sought from a mother is given in the excerpt below (from Moore, 1974, pp. 158–60).

Figure 7 *Example of details of a child's history*

   2. THE COLLECTION OF NECESSARY FACTS
      (Select, expand, modify or omit items as required.)

A. *The Home.* What sort of accommodation—house, part house, flat (what floor)? How many rooms for how many people? Child sleeps in own room/shares with whom? Shares bed?
   Are domestic facilities adequate (own toilet, bath, heating etc.)? Is there a garden or play space? Busy/quiet street?
   Does the home meet the family's needs and are they happy there? If not, any prospect of improvement?

B. *Family and others closely connected.* List (*a*) members of (nuclear) family, with ages, children's names, whether each member living at home or away, and whether at work, at school or neither; (*b*) others living with the family (relatives, au pairs, etc); (*c*) relatives living nearby and seen frequently.

(i) *Father.* Age? Health? Occupation? (settled job? satisfied with it? hours?) How much does he see of the children? How much does he do with them (especially this child)? Anything else volunteered, e.g. about his personality, background, history.

(ii) *Mother.* Age (estimated if necessary)? Health? Present and past occupations?

If at work now does she enjoy it? Hours? Arrangements for children when she is out (including school holidays)? How much does she do with the child?

If she worked when this child was under school age, what arrangements were made? How often did these arrangements change?

If not at work does she wish/plan to start? Feel frustrated?

Anything else volunteered about mother.

How often can parents go out together without the children?

(iii) *Siblings and others in household.* Any serious problems? Contact with child? Anything volunteered.

(iv) *Friends.* Have parents many/few/no friends within reach? Does the child mix freely in the neighbourhood/exchange visits with friends/have none?

(v) *Religion.* Any active religious affiliation of either parent; how does it affect the child?

C. *The child's history*

(i) Pregnancy and birth—any difficulties? Wanted child? Right sex?

(ii) Infancy—healthy baby? Contented or cried a lot? How well did he sleep? Any difficulty with feeding or weaning? Toilet training?

(iii) Any major illnesses? Operations? Accidents? Ever in hospital?—for what, how old, how long? Was he upset at the time or afterwards?

(iv) Any other separations (child away from home without parents, or either parent away for a week or more), how old, how long, with whom, how did he get on at the time, any difficulty afterwards?

(v) How has he taken to any changes in his life (e.g. a new baby, new home, death or departure of any family member, being looked after by someone different)?

(vi) How has he settled and how well has he learnt at each stage of school? (note names of schools, and dates or ages when attended; include nurseries and play groups).

D. *The child now*

(i) General health: good or poor? frequent colds, other ailments?

(ii) What is he like as a person? (cheerful, moody, irritable, nervous, lone wolf, etc.)

(iii) How does he get on with father? With mother? With siblings? With others in household? What happens when he is naughty? How often is punishment necessary? How and by whom punished? How does he take it?

(iv) How does he react if parents disagree about something?

(v) Is he happy at school now; any difficulties there? Are you satisfied with it?

(vi) What does he do in spare time? (interests, activities, pets, bicycle, etc.) Where and with whom does he play?

(In a full length interview it is often useful to administer the Vineland Scale of Social Maturity as a measure of independence training.)

Anything else volunteered.

E. *The problem*

Fill in gaps in the parents' spontaneous account of the problem and any other difficulties by enquiring as necessary about the onset, course and frequency of the behaviour in question, methods tried in dealing with it, its effects on family life, the attitudes of family members, teachers and anyone else concerned, not least the child himself; and if not clear, just what precipitated the referral at this particular time.

What reason was the child given for coming to see the psychologist? (If it seems necessary to correct any false impression he has been given, discussion of the reasons for doing so may provide a useful starting point for an examination of the parents' attitudes to the child and his behaviour, which can be continued in later interviews.)

In Chapter 2 we stressed the importance of recording information immediately it is obtained. It is for this reason that many psychologists regard information which mothers, for example, may provide about their child's early history as information which must necessarily have been distorted. This does not mean that the information must be discarded, but it does mean that its value must be open to question.

It is at about this stage, in the light of the information gained, that the psychologist is likely to be fairly clear on two points. The first is the kinds of behaviours which are causing concern, to whom they cause concern and in what way. The second is the question of whether the psychologist is competent to deal with these behaviours. If the answer to the second question is 'Yes', he would probably want next to see the child in order to consider two further points. The first of these is the question of cause. In the light of the information gained, the psychologist might well have some thoughts as to possible causation. Not all psychologists follow this way of thinking, as we shall see later in this chapter. Irrespective of belief in antecedent 'causes' of behaviour, the second of these two points is that of treatment. The psychologist can now begin to organise his thoughts on how best to deal with the problems which have been presented.

This whole process which we have been considering is often called diagnosis. But it is a diagnostic process which is different from that of the ideal medical diagnosis. It is very rare for a psychologist to be able to isolate one particular cause, analogous to the 'bacillus' which may give rise to a variety of medical symptoms, and then to prescribe a specific treatment, such as an antibiotic which will cause the symptoms to disappear. Psychological problems are very rarely ascribable to single causes; very often they are the effect of a variety of different environmental pressures often existing over a long period of time, to which particular individuals will react in very different ways. And a clear-cut and definable point of commencement is not always to be found. For these reasons, the diagnostic process is, for many psychologists, an on-going process which overlaps and reacts with treatment. The two processes are hardly distinguishable. It is difficult to identify a point at which diagnosis stops and treatment starts, for the psychologist will often be constantly revising his 'diagnosis' in the light of the effects of the treatment procedures he suggests. So in a very real sense the treatment is itself a diagnosis. Careful observation of the way a child responds to, for example, different handling on the part of his mother, a changed method of reading at school, a different structure for the relationships which he can build with his brothers and sisters, the introduction of a new programme of behaviour modification—information of this kind is essential to gain a clearer view of the likely reasons for the behaviour being shown. The information is gained

from activities which can be regarded as examples of the kind of
'low-level' or less rigorous kind of experiment mentioned on p. 19.
They are 'single-case' experiments, aimed at solving immediate
human problems rather than contributing to research literature. But
they none the less involve testing hypotheses by systematically
altering conditions and observing effects. And they exemplify the
overlapping of diagnosis and treatment. The diagnostic process is
well discussed in Wedell (1972), and those who are interested in the
psychologist's approach will find the diagnostic/treatment discussion
handled there.

Treatment itself is broadly based on changing the child's environment, or in effect his experiences. There are three main approaches
which psychologists follow. The approaches are not completely distinct,
and indeed most psychologists are likely to use elements of any one
approach depending on their relative usefulness.

The first treatment approach is the behavioural approach. This
stems largely from the work of B. F. Skinner, who believes in essence
that all behaviour is generated through the action of reward. So
treatment consists of designing a programme of rewards which are
appropriate for the child and which he gains when the desired
behaviour occurs. The behaviour which is disliked is usually ignored
and therefore is not rewarded. This last point is important, since
sometimes even 'telling off' a child for disliked behaviour is in itself a
reward, for the attention generated is something which may be sought
by the child. This is an approach which neglects 'cause' (see p. 25). The
psychologist's main concern is to structure the environment so as to
influence a change in the behaviour; *why* the behaviour arose in the
first place is, to the Skinnerian, a redundant question.

An example of a programme (devised by Professor Howard N.
Sloane, Jr, of the University of Utah, USA), in this case for a child
whose room is particularly untidy, is given below (Peine and Howarth,
1975).

1 Decide upon a time each day when you will check the room. The
   child may or may not be present.
2 Give the child points for the condition of his room. A score of 3
   means the room is tidy, an above average performance; a score of
   2 means the room has just a few things around, and can be
   considered a typical satisfactory performance. A score of 1 means
   the room was pretty messy, and a zero indicates chaos.

3 Put up a chart in the child's room. This should show how many points the child gets each day. Each time you inspect, mark the score on the chart.

4 Decide on some privilege which the child can earn with the points. It may be something the child already receives, such as being allowed to watch TV, or receiving all his pocket money. Make each point worth a certain amount of the privilege.

If the privilege is to be something the child does not already receive regularly, at the beginning select something small enough to be used for frequent rewards. Whatever you use, decide on a specific number of points required for a certain amount of privilege. You may also put on the chart or in the room some indication of the value of the points.

5 Depending on the privilege to be earned, the points may be traded in daily or once a week. The more frequently the better, especially with younger children. It is also quite acceptable to allow the child to trade points in whenever he wishes to and has enough to trade. At the trade-in time add up the points the child has to date, let him trade as many as he wants, and mark the number left on the chart. Points left at the end of a week can be saved for the future; just mark the number of points saved from the previous week or weeks on the new sheets of the chart.

6 Before starting the programme, describe it to the child. Be quite clear in indicating what behaviour will obtain points, and how many points will be earned for different degrees of room tidiness. Explain the trade-in procedure and the privileges which can be earned by points. Make clear that he cannot receive these privileges in any other way. Show him the chart and how it will be filled in. Do not argue, or debate the programme. Describe it, and indicate that you will leave it to him whether or not he wants to clear his room to earn points and privileges. Then do exactly that—leave it to the child.

7 Remember to be consistent when you have decided on a system.

This is very simple programme for a not very serious behaviour problem. More serious behaviour problems usually demand more carefully worked out programmes, with attention being paid to the frequency with which the behaviour occurs. The progress of the programme is then carefully monitored over a period of time, and the behaviour change checked in a systematic way.

A second approach to treatment rests largely on psychoanalytic views. The psychoanalytic school holds that the main characteristics of children's behaviour, and indeed adult behaviour, are largely determined by the early childhood relationships which were formed. Thus Bowlby (1952) has provided evidence for the development of a moral sense in children being related fairly closely to the presence of a stable mother or mother-figure during the years of early childhood. The analysts hold that later personality characteristics are largely due to different sort of early experiences—for example, obsessional, over-careful, fussy behaviour mey be due to an over-rigid and over-precise toilet training by the mother.

It is, of course, not possible to modify these events, which have taken place in the individual's distant past, but it is possible to have some influence on their effects. With older children this is achieved through talking about the experiences, and with younger children who are unable to communicate verbally through a process of 'playing out'. This consists of using the young child's natural means of communication, such as toys, water and sand, as a means of helping him express his feelings; the words which older children and adults use to explain their feelings are often too complicated and sophisticated for him to be able to use.

One of the best descriptions of treatment which follows this kind of psychoanalytical approach in dealing with behaviour problems is given by Virginia Axline (1966), who treated a child named Dibs. Dibs was a very withdrawn but intelligent six-year-old, showing quite bizarre behaviour at school, where he was regarded as a boy of very limited ability. In the excerpt given below Dibs is using the play material to illustrate his feelings about his father, and also trying to explain his feelings to the therapist.*

He picked up the metal shovel and quietly and intently dug a deep hole in the sand. Then I noticed that he had selected and set apart one of the toy soldiers. When he had finished digging the hole he carefully placed that soldier in the bottom of the hole and shovelled sand in on top of it. When the grave was filled in he slapped the top of it with the back of the shovel. 'This one just got buried,' he announced. 'This one did not get a chance to even try to climb that hill. And of course, he did not get to the top. Oh, he

---

*Children's conversation is sometimes very allusive. Ginott (1969 and 1973), is well worth reading on this topic.

wanted to. He wanted to be with the others. He wanted to hope, too. He wanted to try. But he didn't get a chance. He got buried.'

'So that one got buried,' I commented. 'He didn't get a chance to climb up the hill. And he didn't get to the top.'

'He got buried,' Dibs told me, leaning toward me as he spoke, 'and not only did he get buried, but I will build another big, high, powerful hill on the top of that grave. He will never, never, never get out of that grave. He will never, never, never have a chance to climb any hill again!' He scooped up the sand with broad sweeps of his hands and built a hill over the grave he had made—over the grave of the buried toy soldier. When the hill was completed, he brushed the sand from his hands, sat there cross-legged, looking at it. 'That one was Papa,' he said quietly, climbing out of the sandbox.

'It was Papa who got buried under the hill?'

'Yes,' Dibs replied. 'It was Papa.'

The church chimes rang. Dibs counted three chimes as they struck the hour. 'One. Two. Three. Four. Four o'clock,' he said. 'I have a clock at home and can tell time.'

'You have?' I replied. 'And you can tell time, too.'

'Yes,' he said. 'There are many different kinds of clocks. Some you wind. Some are electric. Some have alarms. Some play chimes.'

'And what kind is yours?' I asked. Dibs seemed to be retreating from the burial of 'Papa' by this intellectual discourse. I would go along with him. It would take time for him to work through these feelings about his father. If he seemed to feel that he was getting in over his head, if he seemed to be a little frightened by what he had just played out, and if he sought for himself a retreat into the safety of a discussion about some material things—like clocks—I would not rush him into any probing of his feelings. He had already made some very concise, affective statements in his play.

This extract hardly gives the flavour of a full approach to treatment following this line, and readers who wish to gain further insight into this approach are advised to read the Axline book. In fact, the excerpt given is not as 'interpretative' as would be the case in many analytic treatments: the therapist is not so much giving the child her interpretations of his feelings as accepting his own feelings. To this extent the excerpt shows the influence of Carl Rogers, who is mentioned in the next paragraph.

The third main line of treatment can be characterised as the self-concept approach. Psychologists who follow this approach hold the view that behaviour derives from the view that the individual has of himself, the extent to which he appreciates his own identity and his capacity for changing it. It is believed that discrepancies between an individual's view of himself and the view that others such as his relatives and peers hold of him are very often at the root of the development of inappropriate behaviour. The essence of treatment for psychologists who follow this approach is to help the individual to understand his own self-concept and to achieve a self-concept which is both healthy and realistic. This is largely done through skilled discussion, and therefore is a form of treatment which is much more appropriate for older children than younger ones. The excerpt from a quotation in Bessell (1971) is an example which follows lines advocated by Carl Rogers who, while not directly associated with this school, nevertheless is often used as a model for treatment approaches by psychologists who are believers in the self-concept approach. The excerpt illustrates vividly the way in which this counsellor follows Rogers's line of reflecting the client's own views and feelings so as to avoid directing the client or 'counselee' in any way. The differences between this approach and that of the behaviourists in particular are readily appreciated.

Counselor: The last time we talked you indicated that you were thinking seriously of dropping out of school. Have you given this thought any further consideration?

Counselee: Yes, I have, Dean ... As it is now I still believe that I may drop out of school.

Counselor: You feel that as things are going now you still plan to drop out of school.

Counselee: I think I will because, I don't know, unless something changes so that I can more or less get into the groove of things, I think I will drop out because I'd rather drop out than flunk out.

Counselor: I see. You feel that you'd rather drop out than flunk out. Unless you, uh, you uh, get into the groove as it were.

Counselee: Yes. It seems as if the instructors ae not putting anything in the course. I'm rather disappointed. They are just talking and if you don't want to go to class you don't have to because they are just going straight from the text. They are just going through the motions, as far as I'm concerned.

Counselor: You feel that in some of these classes the instructors are just

going through the motions, as you say, and when you get into a
class you're rather disappointed.

Counselee: Yes, I am, because I figure that here's my chance. I don't
know too much about the subject outside of what I read and I
figure, gee, a professor will start to elaborate on some aspect of the
course and he just rattles on about what the book had already
mentioned—nothing outside. He just goes by the book.

Counselor: And you feel that this is probably an influential factor with
regard to whatever grade you may receive in this particular class?

Counselee: I think so, because it depends—well, if somebody reads the
book and commits it to memory he's going to get a good grade,
but if there are certain things in the book that you don't
understand and the teacher isn't taking the time to explain in class
or even outside of class, it's going to hurt your grade.

Counselor: It's a rather cut-and-dried kind of thing. It's going to hurt
your grade.

Counselee: Yes, it is. It is very cut-and-dried. It gets boring at times. You
wish you could get up and walk out of the class but you don't dare.

Counselor: You feel that you'd like to get up and walk out, but you don't
dare because the instructor has his eyes on you.

Counselee: Right.

Of course, as was said earlier, most psychologists working with
children are fairly eclectic and use the most appropriate line of
treatment for the problem with which they are faced. But whatever
type or types of treatment are used, it is characteristic that
psychologists will pay great attention to feedback from the child, from
his parents, from his school, from his social workers, and use this
information in order to assess not only the effectiveness of treatment,
but also the extent to which the treatment line needs to be changed.
This whole question of success of treatment is a very difficult area to
enter. The evidence on the success or otherwise of psychoanalytic
approaches has been summarised by Levitt (1963), who does not take a
very sanguine view of the relative improvements gained by children who have followed psychotherapy as opposed to children who
were given no treatment at all. But evaluation of something as
delicate and difficult to assess as psychological treatment and
behaviour change can rarely if ever be entirely watertight. The most
rigorous experimentalist may set clear criteria of behaviour change,
only to find that in assessing the objectives which he has set for his

treatment procedure he may have himself brought about other changes which have affected the whole personality and the whole life-style of the child in other, no less important, ways.[1] There is a sense in which the effects of psychological treatment are inestimable in both senses of that word.

This leads to the final point. The kind of approach to working with children which has been outlined in this chapter involves an individual psychologist working with an individual child. But as this book has repeatedly stressed, the wider appreciation by the public of the work of the increased number of psychologists may well lead to a much greater call for their services. This greater awareness by the population of psychological knowledge voices the question: should this greater demand be met by traditional means—steadily increasing the number of psychologists who work in orthodox ways—or should the increasing sensitivity of other members of the community be more utilised, thus enabling other workers with children to use and apply more of the psychologist's skills? This is the theme of the next chapter.

[1] See BERGIN, A. E. (1971) 'The Evaluation of Therapeutic Outcomes', in BERGIN, A. E. and GARFIELD, S. L. (eds.) *Handbook of Psychotherapy and Behaviour Change*. New York: John Wiley.

| Working with children, 2

Put another way, as long as we define the problems of individuals in a way so as to require solution by highly trained professionals, the gap between supply and demand becomes scandalously greater with time.

From 'Community psychology, networks and Mr Everyman', by S. B. Sarason (*American Psychologist*, 31, 5, May 1976)

The growing awareness of childhood as a serious and worth-while subject of study and the consequent steadily increasing interest in the study of children's psychological development was described in Chapter 1. This in turn has produced an increasing demand for psychological services for children. In the 1960s, in response to this demand, the then Ministry of Education established the Summerfield working party to examine the recruitment, training and field of work of educational psychologists and in its report (Department of Education and Science, 1968) the working party made various recommendations relating to a realistic output of educational psychologists. In the event, the growth in the number of educational psychologists employed in local authority school psychological services has been markedly higher than was expected. Figure 7, below, based on Fig 1.2 in Williams (1974), shows how numbers increased over a period from the mid-1950s to the mid 1970s.

Similar pressures have led to the health services employing more clinical psychologists specialising in work with children. And those social services involved with children also seek to employ psychologists for their work. The way in which these different kinds of psychologist collaborate is discussed in the next chapter.

Thus there have been two solutions to the problem of meeting the demands for psychological services for children: the older, more

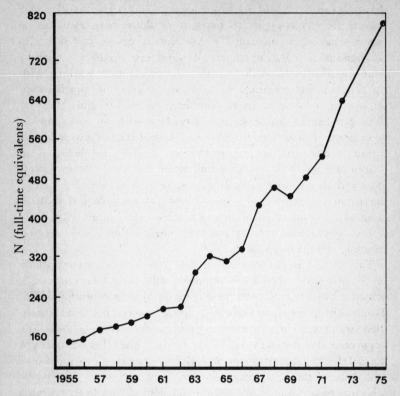

Figure 8 *Educational psychologists in England and Wales 1955–75 (The change between (i) 1962/63 and (ii) 1968/69 are in part accounted for by changes in the system of recording personnel statistics)*

Statistics for England and Wales are now collected separately. The 1975 figure is the combined value of the two separate statistics, obtained through personal communication.

established branch of educational psychology has increased its numbers markedly; in addition, new kinds of psychologists working with children have begun to exist. But these two solutions, both of which lead to a growth in the numbers of psychologists, are not the only ones possible. There are other, more radical ways in which these demands can be met. Many psychologists would argue that one such way is for psychologists to make their skills more available to others—that is, to increase the expertise of others working with children rather than to investigate more and more children themselves. This argument rests on the fact that the psychologist working with children is a highly-trained specialist, whose array of skills is rarely fully brought into play by the problems referred to him. Many of these problems could be satisfactorily dealt with by colleagues in other areas if only they had received a modicum of psychological training; this approach, it is claimed, enables psychologists to concentrate on those questions and issues for which their competence and theirs alone is most appropriate: it would also have a preventative function, since the presence of psychological skills in other workers would enable many problems to be dealt with early, before they grew into serious and long-standing cases needing handling by a psychologist.

This line of argument requires that some of the barriers which professions have erected around their skills should be reduced, a principle which may have been most developed in the educational field. Teachers have, for many years, been given some psychological skills in their training. There are many reasons for this, not least the application that such skills have to the learning and other behaviour of normal children. In addition these skills help teachers identify and deal with some of the behavioural abnormalities in children who might otherwise have required referral to psychologists. This latter reason is most evident in the field of in-service training for teachers. Many experienced teachers take advanced courses in areas such as school counselling, remedial teaching, the education of handicapped children, for example, which are often heavily weighted with psychological (amongst other) skills. Thus a school counselling course would teach a range of skills including those concerned with the developmental problems of adolescence. The trained counsellor would then expect to handle many of these problems in his work, collaborating where appropriate with his psychologist colleague. The counsellor would approach questions from a rather different standpoint and with a different background, but would nevertheless utilize psychological skills for this purpose. The psychologist would only be involved where his expertise was really needed.

Similarly in the health services, the training of nurses and other medical personnel often incorporates a course in psychological techniques and knowledge; training in other fields (for example, social work) also often involves some acquaintance with the principles of such areas of applied psychology as behaviour modification.

In some fields however, the diffusion of psychological skills has been carried further in other ways. Recently Bardon and Bennett (1974) have discussed the ways in which the educational psychologist (or school psychologist in this case) in the United States can be regarded as a behavioural sciences consultant to school personnel. This goes some way beyond work with children and their problems. It is a different approach from that of imparting some knowledge of the psychology of child development and child management. It shifts the focus from the child to those professionals who are themselves concerned with children. Bardon and Bennett argue that in order to work effectively with children there is a case for beginning by working with colleagues who work with children. Consequently the relationships and the administrative procedures which obtain in the school situation are regarded as fair fields in which psychologists with interests in children should make a contribution. This is not just a question of improving teachers' knowledge of children's behaviour. Designing enquiries for schools which will enable better information and record-keeping about children to be carried out, helping school staff to work together to set reasonable and attainable objectives for the school in which they work, improving the personal sensitivity of workers involved with children—these are examples of the kinds of problems over which educational psychologists who work in this way can expect to be consulted.

Not every psychologist would find this kind of work attractive and appealing. There is no direct involvement with children, but there is involvement at a distance, dealing with such considerations as the operations and morale of organisations which are themselves directed towards children. But on the basis that more humane and purposeful schools harbour fewer children with behaviour problems, it can be argued that this is an effective and alternative way of using psychological skills at a time when the numbers of psychologists trained for work with children seem never to satisfy the demand.

In earlier chapters, this book has argued that parents are probably the most important of the psychologists's colleagues. Nevertheless it can be argued that while parents have the richest practical experience of child development, they also have the poorest preparation for child rearing. Parents usually have a close experience of no more than two or

three children (their own) in a lifetime. Unless they are willing, on
their own initiative, to read some of the texts on child development—and there are many parents who would not dream of reading a
book—they are likely to have no background of information and
knowledge against which to set the development of their own children.
They do not know whether a particular child's behaviour is only to be
expected in many children of his age group, or whether it is a very
unusual example of behaviour which needs and deserves attention at
once. The mother of a child who, at the age of eight, was typing a flora
of his village, specialising in grasses, was aware that his behaviour was
somewhat different from other eight-year-olds; her main reaction was
one of gratitude that this interest kept her son quiet when he might have
been demanding attention. The psychologist however was fasci-
nated, knowing something of the rarity of this kind of intellectual
behaviour in eight-year-olds and feeling at once the need to make
available opportunities for nourishing an unusual talent.

Discussions with neighbours and relatives may to some extent widen
the background of information which is available but this may contain
old wives' tales which, as well as being inaccurate, may actually
mislead. Particularly in the era of working mothers, the time available
for parents to find out about the kinds of development they might
expect their children to show is limited. Yet parents are very much at
the 'sharp end' of children's behaviour. The psychologist may advise
the parent to ignore a child's screaming and to reward quiet
behaviour, but it is the parent who has had to sit and stop up his ears
while the screaming proceeds. The psychologist may advise what to do
over a child's delinquent behaviour, but it is the parent who has had to
cope with the angry neighbours or the irritated police. It is in the field
of work with parents that perhaps the psychologists' greatest potential
contribution lies.

A good example of the way in which psychologists can broaden
parents' understanding of their own children's behaviour comes from
work in the field of handicapped children. Here, the Hester Adrian
Centre for the Study of Mental Retardation has developed a course in
child development for parents of slow learning children. The course,
which is really a workshop where parents come for study over a period
of time, includes details of child development norms which are simply
worded so as to avoid technicalities, practical in application and which
parents find helpful. An example of the kind of material provided is
given below, taken from an illustration provided by Mittler (1974).

Child development charts[1]
Compiled by Dorothy Jeffree and Cliff Cunningham
These charts represent only approximate guides to the sequence of development
Introduction to the charts: Peter Mittler

1   The developmental chart is a sequence of stages of normal child development.

2   It is not to be taken too seriously as we cannot realistically compare normal and subnormal, for many reasons, one being that subnormals vary more than normals.

3   The main aims of the chart are:

a to help the parent OBSERVE their own child

b to give sufficient detail of development for parents to view it SYSTEMATICALLY and as a SEQUENCE

c to help parents work out their child's STRENGTHS AND WEAKNESSES in readiness for planning activities.

The chart splits development into specific areas. This is to help us think systematically about development. Some areas may be out of step and lag behind e.g. the physical development of many mongol babies in the first year may not be far behind normal development, but this does not predict later development and parents may be disappointed. We should always end up looking at the whole child and not concentrate on looking at one aspect.

5   The chart attempts to give a detailed and systematic view of normal development so that the *sequences* of development are made more clear. NB: There is no evidence to suggest that these developmental sequences are different in the normal and sub-normal. Both the normal and subnormal sometimes omit stages in a sequence e.g., they may not crawl but walk immediately. Some subnormal children seem to skip a stage because of physical and other handicaps.

6   A knowledge of the sequences will help the parent to chart the child's present level of development. By looking at the next stage of the sequence he can think ahead realistically. This will provide more accurate *expectancies* of his child. In building up these expectancies we must remember that the chart is for normal children. It is only the parents who can say which part is appropriate to their own child.

7   Just as physical handicaps can deprive children of experiences,

[1] Compiled for the National Society for Mentally Handicapped Children (North West Region) and the Hester Adrian Research Centre, University of Manchester: Parents' Workshop 1971

so can lack of a drive to seek out experiences. Parents may be fearful and overprotective and so discourage a child from exploring and finding out.

8   For subnormal even more than for normal children, intelligence seems to develop through physical experiences—e.g. seeing and touching a variety of shapes, sizes, textures and weights, and hearing a variety of sounds. Some of these experiences will be readily available in everyday life, though we often need to organize them for the child who cannot seek them out for himself. Other experiences need more thought.

9   A major difference between the development of the normal and the subnormal is speed. Many aspects of development take a long time to come. We want to ask why they are not appearing and how we can help to bring them about. What we must not do is sit back and wait; we might wait for ever.

10   It is equally bad to try to produce a skill that the child is not ready for. We must try to achieve a BALANCE. By careful observation and a sound knowledge of the developmental sequences, it is possible for the parent realistically to anticipate the child's needs. To summarize ask: a What has the child missed out and why?
                                    b What might he do next?
                                    c How can YOU tackle it?
When doing this use your own judgement, be patient and optimistic.

January 1971   Workshop—NSMHC

1   CHILD'S NAME
                    Christian   Surname
        AGE_____   YEARS_____   MONTHS_____ SEX_____
        Type of handicap (if known)

2   Look at your developmental chart. Estimate the level your child has reached in each area. Write down the rating (i.e. the number given at the side of the level) in the appropriate box.

    A PHYSICAL SKILLS
        1 Head   [_____]
        2 Legs   [_____]
        3 Arms and hands   [_____]
        4 General body movements   [_____]
    B PERFORMANCE   [_____]
    C SOCIAL   [_____]
    D LANGUAGE   [_____]

3   Briefly describe the major problems you have with your child.

PHYSICAL SKILLS [1]

Head

1 Lifts head slightly when lying on tummy.
    Holds head steady for few seconds when held at shoulder.

2 Lifts head when lying on tummy.

3 Lifts head when lying on back.
    Holds head erect and steady when held at shoulder.
    Holds head steady when in sitting position.

4 Lifts head and chest when lying on tummy.
    Holds head erect continuously.

5 Lifts head and shoulders when lying on back.

There follows a list of other physical, performance, social and language skills. Feedback from workshops of this kind has been very good and is discussed in Cunningham and Jeffree (1975).

This offering of psychological skills to other workers is not in itself a new development. What is new is the increasing emphasis which psychologists working with children are currently giving to it. It is a movement which needs to be viewed against the background of the growth of the 'community psychologist' role (Bender, 1976).

Clarke (1974) has set out the aims of the community psychology movement fairly concisely. Many of the problems of our time have been seen as medical problems in which a skilled professional considers the symptoms, identifies the cause of the complaint and recommends a course of treatment. But the supporters of the community movement argue that while this approach may well be very successful in dealing with identifiable disease, such as malaria, it is far less successful in dealing with scourges such as alcoholism, for example. Many alcoholics have been helped to a much greater extent by community organisations such as Alcoholics Anonymous than by their doctor. Sarason (1976) expressed it well 'Put another way, as long as we define the problems of individuals in a way so as to require solution by highly trained professionals, the gap between "supply and demand" becomes scandalously greater with time.'

---

[1] In the left hand column is given the age in months which the behaviour normally appears.

Placing the discussion in the context of children's problems, it is argued that the large numbers of delinquent, maladjusted, slow-learning children might be much better helped if the psychologist devoted his energies to working with the community in which these behaviour patterns appear, placing his own psychological knowledge and skills at the disposal of those community organisations which are concerned with these human problems, collaborating with them in order to redesign the living environment so as to help prevent these difficulties arising. Just as it is better to persuade a community to install a sewage system than to treat its cholera victims, so it may be better to help persuade a community to develop and diversify its youth service and play facilities than to offer psychological help to its delinquents.

So the community psychologist is involved in preventive work with the community. This does not deny the need for the psychologist who works with the individual child. Community work of the sort described will certainly help to prevent problems, but there is no evidence to suggest that it will abolish them, attractive though that prospect is.

It is worth reiterating that psychologists have in the past placed their knowledge of children's growth and behaviour at the service of the community through books, the media, public lectures and so on. The community movement, however, brings the psychologist off the fence of professional neutrality and makes him an active worker in the service of the many pressure groups which want to improve and alter the structure of society. This is a situation which the community psychologist must be prepared to meet.

It will, of course, be foolish to imagine a situation in which every man becomes his own psychologist. There is little doubt that psychologists will be needed for work with individual children for the foreseeable future. Increasing the psychological competence of parents and other colleagues is only one of the various procedures suggested at the beginning of this chapter, and it is complementary to the more orthodox procedure in which the psychologist works directly with the child. There is little evidence as yet of any society relying solely on the newer roles of psychologists, to the exclusion of the older, well-tried procedures. But this discussion of the experimenting with the psychologist's role which is currently afoot leads to a consideration of the relationships between the different kinds of psychologists working with children and the services they offer. It is to this point that we turn in the next chapter.

| The professions of child
psychology

Before I built a wall I'd ask to know
What I was walling in or walling out,
And to whom I was like to give offence.

From 'Mending Wall' by Robert Frost

Not many years ago, few people in Britain would have been able to say
that they had met a psychologist. The word 'psychologist' would have
given rise to a sense of uncertainty and bewilderment in many people.
Coulson (1968) has given some evidence of the misperceptions which
were recently held of the roles of psychologists. The situation was very
different in relation to members of other professions, such as doctors or
teachers, whom everyone would have met on many different occasions.

Today the situation has changed. As psychologists continue to grow
in number, so grows the likelihood of acquaintance with them, and
knowledge of the work that psychologists do is spread through the
community. But as numbers have grown, so have specialisms
developed. Since people are not now likely to meet a psychologist, but
a clinical psychologist or a social psychologist, the sense of bewilderment may well continue. The applied psychologist is now a
graduate in psychology, who holds a post-graduate master's or doctoral
degree in his specialism and who is sometimes required to have had
some years of experience of other work with children as well (e.g.
educational psychologists, who must be experienced teachers). Speciali-
sation of function has value; it also has drawbacks. The purpose of this
chapter is to outline the organization which underpins the different
specialisms in the work of applied psychologists concerned with
children.

Broadly speaking, the study of psychology in establishments of higher education in Britain is organised into areas which reflect research and teaching interests. Psychology graduates will have followed courses in such areas as experimental design, learning, neurological psychology, abnormal psychology, and so on. These areas are not static entities. As new knowledge is generated, the ways in which psychological knowledge can best be structured in the interests of students will alter. Teaching areas develop as a result of the research work and the interests of psychologists trying to understand behaviour, and may not necessarily have direct application to the work of practising psychologists. Irrespective of the kind of course being followed, which will understandably vary, depending to some extent on the research interests of the institution and staff, the successful undergraduate emerges from his studies with a degree in psychology. With this qualification, in Britain he is eligible to apply for graduate membership of the British Psychological Society, where the organisation is somewhat different. Not only is the Society organised into sections, reflecting the various areas into which psychological knowledge and interest can be structured, it also has superimposed on its membership a divisional organisation which represents the interests of members working in particular applied fields.

This alternative organisation can be held to reflect current applications of psychology to the needs of the community. Psychologists work for different kinds of employers. The Education Service is a large employer, and presently probably the biggest. Nearly all educational psychologists work in Local Education Authorities. The Health Service is another large employer of psychologists. As the British Psychological Society (1973) said in a report: 'Clinical Psychology is a relatively small but rapidly growing profession which has developed alongside the National Health Service.' It is not surprising that nearly all clinical psychologists work in the National Health Service. The Employment Services also use the services of psychologists who are usually referred to as occupational or vocational psychologists. Each of these fields of applied psychology has a divisional organisation to represent its interests in the British Psychological Society.

The needs of the applied fields have themselves had repercussions on the structure of departments of psychology in institutions of higher education. Many teaching departments now run post-graduate courses in the applied fields for their graduates. So in various institutions of higher education, courses leading to post-graduate qualifications in educational psychology, clinical psychology, occupational psychology and so on have been established. The organisation of postgraduate courses is very much that of the divisions, or applied fields, whereas the organisation of undergraduate courses is very much that of the sections, or academic research fields. And it is the applied fields which give their names to the psychologists whom administrators, teachers, parents, social workers and others are likely to meet. What is the relationship between these groups of psychologists? Consider the following problem, taken from a real situation.

John was twelve years of age, with a history of epilepsy. His headmaster had invited his mother to school to discuss John's great reading difficulties—his reading skills were approximately those of an eight-year-old and the headmaster proposed that the educational psychologist should be asked to take the case on as a matter of urgency.

In discussing John with the headmaster, his mother pointed out that he was under the care of a local medical specialist for his epilepsy and that he had done a lot of tests with the psychologist at the hospital. What she herself was really worried about was not the reading itself, but the kind of job which would be suitable for a boy with John's medical history and school problems.

Which psychologist is best equipped to deal with John's problem? Should it be an educational psychologist, since the problem is educational? Should it continue to be a clinical psychologist, since the problem has medical overtones and the young person is already in touch with a hospital? Should it be an occupational psychologist, because the concern about the kind of future employment is obviously one of the very strong factors, if not the strongest factor, in the situation? Or should it be all three? If all these kinds of applied psychologists are to be involved in problems of this kind, will there not be wasteful overlap in their training? It is questions such as these, occurring at all ages, which lead psychologists to consider alternative kinds of approaches to specialisms in applied psychology. Originally, the study of human behaviour was divided by academic interest. Now, in the United Kingdom it is divided into an organisation parallel to that of state or local government departments. There is a case for an alternative organisation, dividing the study of behaviour into periods bounded by developmental stages. For example, applied psychologists could first be divided into child psychologists and adult psychologists. Child psychologists could be further sub-divided into family psychologists, concerned with very young children, whose world is largely that of the family; school psychologists, concerned with the child from the time his world changes at entry to school until he becomes of school leaving age; and adolescent psychologists, concerned with counselling and guiding young persons from school-leaving age until the end of their teens. The employing authorities of these different psychologists would then be relatively unimportant. What would matter, it can be argued, would be the skills which they could deploy to cover the needs of the particular age groups with which they are working.

This is one kind of alternative structure of professional psychologists working with children. There would be implications for the kind of training which the psychologist has. Training arrangements would not be affected by the kind of government department or local authority unit in which psychologists work, but would be dictated much more by the needs of the age group with which the particular psychologist was specialising. This is not to say that the special considerations (e.g. legislation, terms of reference, background, and so on) of the different employing organisations would be neglected. These can be seen as important but not major considerations in framing a training syllabus.

In this way, the problems of the overlap and duplication in training of the different kinds of psychologists might well be eased. But this would in turn lead to duplication of a different sort. It could be argued that the school psychologist could not really do his job without knowledge of the work and experience of the family psychologist, nor could he adequately discuss the school careers of his clients without some knowledge of the field of expertise of the adolescent psychologist. Conversely, how could the family psychologist operate when his main referrals would probably be young handicapped children whose parents ask primarily for information and reassurance over the educational and vocational futures of their children (Anderson, 1973)? These questions would lie in the province of the school psychologists and vocational psychologists. So, some problems would be solved at the expense of creating others.

Any system of specialisms poses difficulties, however organised. Another factor which is of relevance to the specialism issue can best be illustrated from the field of education. The expansion of knowledge about all aspects of the growth and development of child behaviour is a well known phenomenon (Dubin, 1972). But the expansion of our knowledge relating to the behaviour of children learning in the school situation is vast indeed. It is one of the reasons that have led Biggs (1976b) to suggest that we coin the term 'educology' to describe this and acknowledge its separation from psychology.

These is, in the author's view, much to be said for experimenting with the point of view set out by Biggs and teaching the area outlined as a first degree subject, though whether it could best be described as leading to a degree in educology or educational psychology is a matter outside the scope of this book. The point being made here is that new knowledge is forcing teaching which had hitherto been placed at post-graduate level into the undergraduate syllabus, which leads to specialisms being recognised earlier. This is currently happening over knowledge being generated at the boundaries of two disciplines (in this case psychology and education), as happened a century or more ago when psychology itself began to grow from that troubled boundary between the philosophers and biologists, studying human behaviour from different territories.

The pressures leading to earlier and more specialisms are forces which it will be difficult to ignore. Already in Britain there are calls for a new specialism of applied child psychologist (Berger, 1975). In the USA the specialism of clinical child psychology is already established and in turn is having to ponder the formation of a separate specialism of paediatric psychology (Tuma, 1975), characterised by the location of its member's work—that is, with children in hospital-based paediatric wards and clinics, and not by age-range or kind of problem.

In several countries an additional specialism is being established, that of the community psychologist (Bender, 1976; Clarke, 1974; Sarason, 1976) mentioned in Chapter 6. Like the traditional special-isms, it is again the location of the psychologist's work, in this case community organisations, which gives the specialism its name. But again, the community psychologist has the alleviation or even the prevention of some children's problems as one of his objectives. The essential point is that the number of specialisms is increasing as are the memberships of the older specialisms, leading to the much greater likelihood of their activities and methods overlapping. Indeed, in a literal as well as a metaphorical sense psychologists working with children will meet in that ill-defined area, the community.

It is the growing size of the profession that will enable them to do this. When psychologists were few and far between, irrespective of the occupation that they held, the need for professional collaboration was small. It is only 30 years ago that there were no more than a hundred or so applied psychologists of all kinds working in England and Wales. In those days the likelihood of an educational psychologist working in a school system coming into professional contact with a clinical psychologist working in a hospital was remote indeed. But today the situation is entirely different. The knowledge of child development, children's needs, children's learning, which all psychologists require is something which all will have had to a greater or lesser extent in their training courses. All psychologists will be moving out to disperse their psychological skills among the population at large. This will have to be done on a collaborative basis. And it will require not merely collaboration between specialisms. It will require collaboration between psychologists and many of their organisations. It will not be possible to change psychologist's roles, and work intensively through the community, without the community itself claiming some influence over the kinds of skill that it will need its psychologists to deploy.

Collaboration between specialisms does not mean that there will necessarily be a unified applied child psychology profession as advocated by Berger. The time for that probably passed when the old Committee of Professional Psychologists (Mental Health) of the British Psychological Society decided to divide itself into an education and a health section as opposed to an adult and a child section. But it may well be time for those psychologists working with children to form a federation of applied child psychologists with some collaborative scheme for influencing the content and scope of the training arrangements which lead to their qualification. A federation could include not only those specialisms such as educational psychology and clinical child psychology but all applied psychologists who work with children irrespective of the kind of specialism they offer. These are the psychologists who will increasingly have to collaborate in their work. It will be important to reinforce each other and to understand each other. For understanding each other will enable the community at large—the lay community—itself to understand the work that applied child psychologists, of whatever persuasion, carry out.

References

ANDERSON, E. M. (1973) *The Disabled School Child: A Study of Interaction in Primary Schools*. London: Methuen.

ARIES, P. (1962) *Centuries of Childhood*. New York: Alfred A. Knopf; London: Cape.

AXLINE, V. (1966) *Dibs: In Search of Self*. London: Gollancz; also Harmondsworth: Penguin (1971).

BALL, S. and BOGATZ, G. A. (1970) *The First Year of Sesame Street: An Evaluation*. Princeton, New Jersey: Educational Testing Service.

BARDON, J. I. and BENNETT, V. C. (1974) *School Psychology*. Englewood Cliffs, New Jersey: Prentice Hall.

BAYLEY, N. (1949) 'Consistency and Variability in the Growth of Intelligence from Birth to Eighteen Years'. *J. gen. Psychol.*, 75, pp. 165–96.

BENDER, M. (1976) *Community Psychology*. London: Methuen.

BERGER, M. (1975) 'Clinical Psychology Services for Children'. *Bull. Br. psychol. Soc.*, 28, pp. 102–7.

BESSELL, R. (1971) *Interviewing and Counselling*. London: Batsford.

BIGGS, J. B. (1976a) 'Schooling and Moral Development', in VARMA, V. and WILLIAMS, P. (eds.) *Piaget, Psychology and Education*. London: Hodder and Stoughton, pp. 155–71.

BIGGS, J. B. (1976b) 'Wanted: A New Discipline'. *Australian Psychologist*, 1, pp. 43–52.

BLACKHAM, G. J. and SILBERMAN, A. (1975) *Modification of Child Behaviour*, 2nd edition. Belmont, Calif.: Wadsworth Publishing Co.

BLOOM, B. S. (1964) *Stability and Change in Human Characteristics*. New York: John Wiley.

BOWLBY, J. (1952) *Maternal Care and Mental Health*. Geneva: World Health Organisation.

BRITISH PSYCHOLOGICAL SOCIETY (1973) 'Report on the Role of Psychologists in the Health Service'. *Bull. Br. psychol. Soc.*, 26, pp. 309–30.

BRONFENBRENNER, U. (1974) *Is Early Intervention Effective?* Vol. 2 of *Report on Longitudinal Evaluation of Pre-school Programmes.* Washington, D.C.: U.S. Department of Health.

BURT, C. (1957) *The Causes and Treatment of Backwardness,* 4th edition. London: University of London Press Ltd.

CAULFIELD, E. J. (1931) *The Infant Welfare Movement in the Eighteenth Century.* New York: Hoeber.

CAVENAGH, F. (ed.) (1931) *James and John Stuart Mill on Education.* Cambridge: Cambridge University Press.

CHAZAN, M. (in press) 'Social Adjustment', in CHAZAN, M. and WILLIAMS, P. (eds.) *Deprivation and the Infant School.* Oxford: Blackwell.

CLARKE, A. D. B. and CLARKE, A. M. (1972) 'Consistency and Variability in the Growth of Human Characteristics', in WALL, W. D. and VARMA, V. (eds.) *Advances in Educational Psychology 1.* London: Hodder and Stoughton, pp. 32–52.

CLARKE, A. M. (1974) 'Community Health Care: Implications for Psychologists and for Society'. *Australian Psychologist,* 9, Monograph Supplement No. 1.

CLARKE, A. M. and CLARKE, A. D. B. (1976) *Early Experience: Myth and Evidence.* London: Open Books, pp. 27–66.

COULSON, N. (1968) 'Some Working-class and Middle-class Ideas on Child Guidance Clinics, Educational Psychologists and IQ'. *Association of Educational Psychologists' Newsletter* No. 10, January 1968, pp. 16–18.

COX, T. (in press) 'Language Skills', in CHAZAN, M. and WILLIAMS, P. (eds.) *Deprivation and the Infant School.* Oxford : Blackwell.

CUNNINGHAM, C. C. and JEFFREE, D. M. (1975) 'The Organisation and Structure of Workshops for Parents of Mentally Handicapped Children'. *Bull. Br. psychol. Soc.,* 28, pp. 405–11.

DARWIN, C. (1873) *The Expression of the Emotions in Man and Animals.* London: Murray.

DARWIN, C. (1877) 'Autobiographical Sketch of an Infant'. *Mind,* ii, 7, pp. 285–94.

DAVIE, R., BUTLER, N. and GOLDSTEIN, H. (1972) *From Birth to Seven.* London: Longman.

DAVIES, P. and WILLIAMS, P. (1975) *Aspects of Early Reading Growth.* Oxford: Blackwell.

DEPARTMENT OF EDUCATION AND SCIENCE (1967) *Children and their Primary Schools* (The Plowden Report). London: H.M.S.O.

DEPARTMENT OF EDUCATION AND SCIENCE (1968) *Psychologists in Education Services* (The Summerfield Report). London: H.M.S.O.

DEUTSCH, M. (1965) 'The Role of Social Class in Language Development and Cognition'. *Amer. J. Orthopsychiat.*, 35, pp. 78–88.

DOUGLAS, J. W. B. (1966) *The Home and the School.* London: MacGibbon and Kee.

DUBIN, S. S. (1972) 'Obsolescence of Life-long Education'. *Am. Psychol.*, 27, 5, pp. 486–98.

FLEMING, C. M. (1969) *Manual to Kelvin Measurement of Ability in Infant Classes.* Glasgow: Robert Gibson.

FOGELMAN, K. B. (1970) *Piagetian Tests for the Primary School.* Slough: N.F.E.R.

FRASER, E. (1959) *Home Environment and the School.* London: Hodder and Stoughton.

GINOTT, H. G. (1969), *Between Parent and Child: New Solutions to Old Problems,* new edition. London: Staples.

GINOTT, H. G. (1973) *Between Parent and Teenager,* revised edition. London: Cassell.

HALSEY, A. H. (ed.) (1972) *Educational Priority: Report of a Research Project sponsored by the Department of Education and Science and the Social Science Research Council, Vol. 1: E.P.A. Problems and Policies.* London: H.M.S.O.

HARRIS, D. B. (1963) *Children's Drawings as Measures of Intellectual Maturity. A Revision and Extension of the Goodenough Draw-a-man Test.* New York: Harcourt Brace and World.

HEARNSHAW, L. S. (1964) *A Short History of British Psychology, 1840–1940.* London: Methuen.

HEBER, R. and GARBER, H. (1975) 'Progress Report II: An Experiment in the Prevention of Cultural-Familial Retardation', in PRIMROSE, D. A. (ed.) *Proceedings of the Third Congress of the International Association for the Scientific Study of Mental Deficiency, Vol. i.* Warsaw: Polish Medical Publishers, pp. 34–43.

HERBERT, G. W. (1974) 'Teachers' Ratings of Classroom Behaviour: Factorial Structure'. *Br. J. educ. Psychol.*, 44, 3, pp. 233–40.

HONZIK, M. P., MACFARLANE, J. W. and ALLEN, L. (1948)"The Stability of Mental Mental Test Performance between Two and Eighteen Years of Age'. *J. Experimental Education*, 17, pp. 309–24.

HYDE, E. M. (1975) 'School Psychological Referrals in an Inner City School'. *Psychology in the Schools*, xii, 4, pp. 412–20.

INHELDER, B. and PIAGET, J. (1958) *The Growth of Logical Thinking from Childhood to Adolescence*, translated PARSONS, A. and MILGRAM, S. London : Routledge and Kegan Paul; New York : Basic Books.

JENCKS, C. (1972) *Inequality*. New York: Basic Books.

KAGAN, J. and MOSS, H. A. (1962) *From Birth to Maturity*. New York: John Wiley.

KAMIN, L. (1974) *Science and Politics of IQ.* New York: Halstead Press.

KANNER, L. (1957) *Child Psychiatry*, 3rd edition. Springfield, Ill.: Thomas.

KERLINGER, F. N. (1973) *Foundations of Behavioural Research*, 2nd edition. New York: Holt, Rinehart and Winston.

LAING, A. F. (1971) 'The Construction of an Infant School Amenities Index'. *Brit. J. educ. Psychol.*, 41, 1, pp. 94–5.

LEVITT, E. E. (1963) 'Psychotherapy with Children: A Further Evaluation'. *Behav. Res. Ther.*, 1, pp. 45–51.

MCKINNON, D. (1976) *Social Class and Educational Attainment: A Summary of Selected Research Reports.* Unpublished supplementary material from *Personality and Learning*, Course E201. Milton Keynes: Open University Press.

MINISTRY OF EDUCATION (1955) *Report of the Committee on Maladjusted Children* (The Underwood Report). London: H.M.S.O., p. 156.

MITTLER, P. (1974) *Growing up with a Disability*. Unit 3 of 'The Handicapped Person in the Community', Course P853. Milton Keynes: Open University Press.

MITTLER, P. (various dates) *Reports on Research at the Hester Adrian Centre*. Unpublished documents, Hester Adrian Centre, University of Manchester.

MOORE, T. (1966) 'Difficulties of the Ordinary Child in Adjusting to Primary School'. *J. child Psychol. Psychiat.*, 7, 1, pp. 17–38.

MOORE, T. (1974) 'The Educational Psychologist and Parents', in CHAZAN, M., MOORE, T., WILLIAMS, P. and WRIGHT, H. J. *The Practice of Educational Psychology*. Harlow: Longman, pp. 148–70.

MUSSEN, P. H. (ed.) (1960) *Handbook of Research Methods in Child Development*. New York: John Wiley.

PEAKER, G. F. (1967) 'The Regression Analyses of the National Survey', in Department of Education and Science *Children and their Primary Schools* (The Plowden Report), Vol. 2, Appendix 4, para. 26 (1), p. 188. London: H.M.S.O.

PEINE, H. A. and HOWARTH, R. (1975) *Children and Parents: Everyday Problems of Behaviour.* Harmondsworth: Penguin.

PHAIRE, T. (1544) *The Boke of Children,* quoted in PINCHBECK, I. and HEWITT, M.(1969) *Children in English Society, Vol. 1*: From Tudor Times to the Eighteenth Century. London: Routledge and Kegan Paul.

PHILLIPS, C. J. (1971) 'Summerfield and After: The Training of Educational Psychologists'. *Bull. Br. psychol. Soc.,* 24, pp. 207–12.

PHILLIPS, J. L. (1969) *The Origins of Intellect: Piaget's Theory.* San Francisco, Calif.: Freeman.

PIAGET, J. (1974) 'The Future of Developmental Child Psychology'. *J. Youth and Adolescence,* 3 (2), pp. 87–93.

RUTTER, M. (1975) *Helping Troubled Children.* Harmondsworth: Penguin.

RUTTER, M., LEBOVICI, S., EISENBERG, L., SNEZNEVSKII, A. V., SADOUN, R., BROOKE, E. and TSUNG-YI LIN (1969) 'A Tri-axial Classification of Mental Disorders in Childhood: An International Study'. *J. child Psychol. Psychiat.,* 10, pp. 41–61.

RUTTER, M., TIZARD, J. and WHITMORE, K. (eds.) (1970) *Education, Health and Behaviour.* Harlow: Longman.

SARASON, S. B. (1976) 'Community Psychology, Networks and Mr Everyman'. *Am. Psychol.,* 31, 5, May 1976, pp. 317–28.

SHEPHERD, M., OPPENHEIM, B. and MITCHELL, S. (1971) *Childhood Behaviour and Mental Health.* London: University of London Press Ltd.

TANNER, J. M. (1961) *Education and Physical Growth.* London: Hodder and Stoughton.

TERMAN, L. M. (ed.) (1959–60) *Genetic Studies of Genius, Vols. 4 and 5.* Stanford, Calif.: Stanford University Press.

TUMA, J. M.(1975) 'Pediatric Psychologist . . . ? Do you mean Clinical Child Psychologist?' *J. Clinical Child Psychology,* Fall 1975, pp 9–12.

VERNON, P. E. (1976) 'Environment and Intelligence', in VARMA, V. and WILLIAMS, P. (eds.) *Piaget, Psychology and Education.* London: Hodder and Stoughton, pp. 31–42.

WARNER, F. (1890) *Lectures on Mental Faculty,* quoted in BURT, C. (1957) *The Causes and Treatment of Backwardness,* 4th edition. London: University of London Press Ltd.

WEDELL, K. (1972) 'Diagnosing Learning Difficulties: A Sequential Strategy', in REID, J. F. (ed.) *Reading: Problems and Practices.* London: Ward Lock.

WHITEHEAD, J. and WILLIAMS, P. (1976) 'Teachers' Preceptions of Children's Behaviour: A Partial Replication of the Wickman Study'. Unpublished study.

WILLIAMS, P. (1974) 'The Growth and Scope of the School Psychological Service', in CHAZAN, M., MOORE, T., WILLIAMS, P. and WRIGHT, H. J. *The Practice of Educational Psychology.* Harlow: Longman, p. 8.

WISEMAN, S. (1964) *Education and Environment.* Manchester: Manchester University Press.

WRIGHT, H. F. (1967) *Recording and Analyzing Child Behaviour with Ecological Data from an American Town.* New York: Harper and Row.

WRIGHT, H. J. (1974) 'Principles in Practice', in CHAZAN, M., MOORE, T., WILLIAMS, P. and WRIGHT, H. J. *The Practice of Educational Psychology.* Harlow : Longman, pp. 308–33.

INDEX

Anderson, E. M., 78, 81
Aries, P., 3, 81
Axline, V., 61–2, 81

Bain, A., 5
Ball, S., 47, 81
Bardon, J. I., 69, 81
Bayley, N., 9, 81
behaviour
  as cause of concern, 13, 30, 32–4, 53, 58, 68
  as symptom of maladjustment, 31–2
  home/school, difference between, 37
  management, 13, 14
  modification, 2, 34, 58, 64–5, 69
    programme, 59–60
  questionnaire, 54–5, 55–7
  rating (Herbert), 35
  study, 1, 28–38, 76, 78
  'worrying', 36
behavioural approach (to treatment), 59–60
Bender, M., 73, 79, 81
Bennett, V. C., 69, 81
Berger, M., 79, 80, 81
Bessell, R., 63, 81
Biggs, J. B., 44, 79, 81
Blackham, G. J., 34, 81
Bloom, B. S., 8, 10, 81
Bogatz, G. A., 47, 81
Bowlby, J., 61, 81
Bronfenbrenner, U., 12, 82
Brown, T., 5
Burt, C., 4, 15, 82

Caulfield, E. J., 3, 82
Cavenagh, F., 43, 82
Chazan, M., 38, 82
child guidance clinics, 30–1, 38, 66
child psychiatry, 3, 30
child study, 5, 6, 7–10, 12, 15–26, 38
child study movement, 5, 6, 28
Clarke, A. D. B., 8, 43, 82
Clarke, A. M., 8, 43, 73, 79, 82
compensatory education, see education
Coulson, N., 75, 82
Cox, T., 12, 82
cross-sectional studies, 23, 24, 25, 35
Cunningham, C., 71, 73, 82

Darwin, C., 2, 5, 15, 16, 21, 22, 23, 28, 82
Davie, R., 10, 12, 82
Davies, P., 24, 82
de Montbeillard, Count P., 16, 23
Deutsch, M., 12, 83
developmental problems
  Isle of Wight survey, 35
  of adolescence, 68
diagnostic process, 53–9
Douglas, J. W. B., 12, 83
Down's Syndrome, 42, 44, 71
Dubin, S. S., 79, 83

education, 5, 6
  compensatory, 12–13
  compulsory, 4, 5, 28–9
  of children with learning difficulties, 5
environment, 4, 11, 12, 26, 40–4, 58, 74
  home, 44–6, 47, 48
  school, 46–7, 48
  social, 47, 48

Fleming, C. M., 17, 83
Fogelman, K. B., 21, 83
Fraser, E., 12, 83

Garber, H., 13, 83
Ginott, H. G., 61, 83

Halsey, A. H., 26, 83
handicapped children: development charts, 70–3
Harris, D. B., 22, 83
Headstart, 42–3
Hearnshaw, L. S., 5, 83
Heber, R., 13, 83
Herbert, G. W., 34, 35, 83
hereditary influences, 40–3, 44, 48
Hester Adrian Research Centre, 44, 70, 71
home, see environment
Honzik, M. P., 9, 83
Howarth, R., 59, 85
Hyde, E. M., 38, 83

individual study (of child), 13, 48, 49–65
Inhelder, B., 19–20, 84
intelligence, 9, 41

Jeffree, D., 71, 73, 82
Jencks, C., 42, 84

Kagan, J., 10, 84
Kamin, L., 41, 84
Kanner, L., 3, 84
Kelinger, F. N., 49, 84

Laing, A. F., 46, 84
language, 6, 12
Levitt, E. E., 64, 84
longitudinal study, 7–8, 9, 10, 11, 19, 21,
    23, 24, 25, 34

McKinnon, D., 12, 46, 84
measurement, 11
    controlled, 16, 17–18, 19, 22, 26
    of home environment, 45–6
méthode clinique, 19, 25, 26
Mill, James, 5, 43
Mill, John Stuart, 4, 43
Mittler, P., 44, 70, 71, 84
Moore, T., 38, 55–7, 84
Moss, H. A. 10, 84
Mussen, P. H., 49, 84

National Child Development Study, 10,
    12, 21, 34

parents
    and child behaviour, 21, 32–4, 36,
      37–8
    and child development charts
      (handicapped children), 71–3
    and knowledge of child development,
      9, 51, 53, 69–70, 74
    and referrals to psychologists, 51
    as colleagues of psychologist, 54, 69–70
    as observers, 50
    attitudes of, 12, 47
    questionnaire involving a mother, 55–7
Peaker, G. F., 47, 48, 84
Peine, H. A., 59, 85
Phaire, T., 2, 85
Phillips, C. J. 13, 85
Phillips, J. L., 19, 85
Piaget, J., 7, 19–20, 84, 85
'playing out', 61–2
Plowden Report, 45, 47, 82
psychoanalytic approach (to treatment),
    61–2, 64
psychological skills, extension of to others,
    68, 73–4
    to parents, 69–70

psychologists
    alternative structure for, 78
    and adolescents, 5, 10
    and referral rate, regional variation in, 38
    community, 73–4, 79, 80
    educational, 75, 76, 77
    in Education Service, 76
    in Employment Service, 76
    in Health Service, 76
    training of, 76, 77, 79, 80

Rogers, C., 62, 63
Rutter, M., 28, 34, 35, 85

Sarason, S. B., 73, 79, 85
school counselling, 68, 69 (in USA)
school psychological service, 26, 29, 30–1,
    66, 67
self-concept approach (to treatment), 62–4
Shepherd, M., 29, 32, 33 (table), 36 (and
    diagram), 37 (and table), 38, 54–5,
    85
Silberman, A., 34, 81
Skinner, B. F., 59
Sloane, H. N., Jr, 59–60
Sully, J., 6, 28
Summerfield committee/Report, 38, 51,
    52, 66, 83

Tanner, J. M., 24, 85
teachers, 13, 21, 29, 30, 34–5, 37–8, 44,
    50, 51, 53, 68
Terman, L., 9, 23, 85
Tizard, J., 35, 85
treatment processes, 50, 59–65
    behavioural, 59–60
    psychoanalytic, 61–2, 64
    self-concept, 62–4
treatment rate, regional variation in, 39
Tuma, J. M., 79, 85
twins, studies of, 41

Underwood committee/Report, 31–2, 84

Vernon, P. E., 42, 85
vocabularies (reading), 24–5

Warner, F., 4, 29, 85
Wedell, K., 59, 86
Whitehead, J., 35, 86
Whitmore, K., 35, 85
Williams, P., 24, 35, 66, 82, 86
Wiseman, S., 12, 86
Wright, H. F., 19, 86
Wright, H. J., 29, 86